D1614001

THE PEARL AND BEAD BOUTIQUE BOOK

**By the same author
and published by Hearthside**

*The Art of Making Bead Flowers
and Bouquets* (1967)
*New Patterns for Bead Flowers
and Decorations* (1969)

The Pearl and Bead Boutique Book

by Virginia Nathanson

Black and white photos by Rex Nathanson

Color photos by Harvey Dresner

Drawings by Carol Nelson

HEARTHSIDE PRESS INC. PUBLISHERS
GREAT NECK, NEW YORK 11021

Contents

Dedication and Acknowledgments

Dedicated to the two most important men in my life, my sons Rex and Brad, and to my dear sister Irene.

Need I mention that there were other pairs of hands to patiently test patterns and expertly duplicate the seemingly endless parts needed for the more ambitious projects? By releasing me from many chores and leaving me free to create and design, a wonderful octet helped "get this show on the road." I am extremely grateful to my talented band: Carolyn Jones, Helen Steibler, Eleanor Fermano, Helen Fink, Faye Shapiro, Mary Sexauer, Lillian Seigal and Mercedes Brill. And I give a special bow to Viola Greenberg, for her role in inspiring and encouraging me.

SHOWN ON JACKET:

Crocheted bolero, p. 40; belt, p. 35; necktie, p. 21; lampshade, p. 172; fuchsias, p. 137; jeweled chains, p. 89-92; pearl bracelet, p. 87; choker and rope necklace, p. 97; crocheted belt, p. 19; Moroccan necklace, p. 73; key chain, p. 129; Sputnik earrings, p. 95; pearl bib, p. 56; crocheted necklaces, p. 12; orange blossom necklace, p. 123; crocheted necklaces, p. 13; braided pearl and gold belt, p. 81; pearl bracelet, p. 15; sachet bag, p. 28; Primrose earrings, p. 126; daisy earrings, p. 123; key chain, p. 130; dome rings, p. 15, pearl belt (see rope belt) p. 19; necklace, p. 61.

INTRODUCTION

The look of the 70s? Morning, noon and night, beads seem to be the answer. There are no rules for what to wear, where. Whatever you want to put together with your own imagination and flair is today's style. The emphasis is definitely on beads whether they are for home or personal adornment, and in the chapters that follow there are designs and patterns for both. I hope they will inspire you to go on with ideas of your own once you are aware of the craftsmanship and materials involved. Those items of costume jewelry that have been gathering dust for years will, most likely, take on a new meaning because they are rich with possibilities. Take them apart, restyle them, combine them with beads and bangles that have a newer look. In other words, have fun! Indeed, I have done just that. It has been great fun tinkering with tiny jewelry findings and weaving in and out of beads with needles, exploring new fields of materials and allowing my imagination to flourish. My new book certainly would not be complete without a fair representation of my first love, the beaded flowers, but as long as I am creating with beads, no matter what kind or size, I am content.

The book is divided into four chapters and each one starts with its own general instructions that include materials and tools required and all the little helpful hints I can pass on to you.

My mailman still brings me thousands of letters each year. Many include color photographs of arrangements made by the sender. Others ask about materials and arranging, but most write just to let me know how happy they are doing bead work.

While compiling materials for this book, I have been aware that I will be addressing women whose know-how ranges from rank beginner to near-Pro in craft and hobby work. If you are a beginner, it will be my pleasure to introduce you to new and fascinating art forms, first with simple instructions and techniques, then gradually, as your dexterity develops, lead you to more complicated projects.

Because some of your first attempts will be easy at the start, they will be no less attractive than the more complicated ones aimed at those of you who are more experienced in working with your hands. For more advanced students there are new patterns and methods and fresh adaptations of some covered in my two previous books. Regarding bead flowers, the new techniques emulate Mother Nature's own creations as closely as possible.

I realize that many of you will have queries regarding individual difficulties. Because of my personal contact with hundreds of students over the years, the problems·solved were wide in scope. My original offer which I made in *The Art of Making Bead Flowers and Bouquets,* and *New Patterns for Bead Flowers and Decorations,* still stands, Please feel free to write to me in care of my publishers if you have any questions. Enclose a large, self-addressed, stamped envelope and I will be delighted to answer as soon as possible.

I have attempted to create the atmosphere of a classroom "workshop" when giving the instructions, and hearing from you by mail makes you all active participants. May the following projects bring you many happy hours of creative pleasure.

I CROCHETING WITH PEARLS AND BEADS

The patterns in this chapter use fairly simple crochet stitches. If you do not know how to crochet, I suggest that you practice the basic stitiches mentioned below, one at a time, and without beads, until you are familiar with each of them. If you do the actual working of the different patterns without beads you will learn more quickly.

Use a fairly large crochet hook (plastic 5 or F), and either 3- or 4-ply wool yarn for your practice pieces to enable you to follow more clearly the directions of the threads and the construction of the design as you work these large patterns. Later you can use the usual fine crocheting threads and smaller hook. To make things easier for you, no abbreviations are given in the stitch directions.

Position of Hands and Holding the Hook

Begin with a loop of thread on the hook. Holding the open end of the thread in the left hand between thumb and first finger, wrap the open end of the thread over and around all four fingers of the left hand spread slightly apart. This will make a circle of the thread. Grasp the thread from the ball, between the thumb and first finger. *Fig. 1*. Holding the hook in the right hand, as you would a pencil, insert the hook end into the center of the circle of thread. *Fig. 2*. With the ball thread over the hook, pull the thread back through the center of the circle of thread, and release the loop. Pull the ball thread until the loop of thread on the hook forms a fairly tight knot.

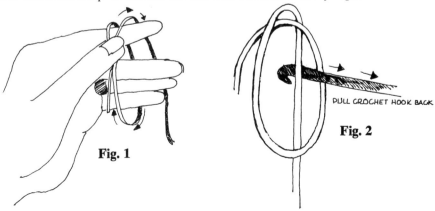

PULL CROCHET HOOK BACK

Fig. 2

Fig. 1

Chain Stitch

Almost all crochet patterns start with a basic chain stitch, the foundation on which all stitches are built. Still holding the hook in the right hand, position the thread from the ball on the left hand by passing it over the first and second fingers, under the ring finger, and over and around the little finger. If the thread is draped loosely in this fashion, the thread will flow easily from the ball, but you will still have enough control over the tension. Hold the loop that is on the hook between thumb and middle finger of your left hand, and separate the fingers slightly. *Fig. 3*. Cross the thread over the hook, *Fig. 4*, and draw the hook and thread through the loop on the hook. This will form one chain stitch. Continue making chain stitches until the stitch feels easy for you. With practice, the size of the stitch will become uniform. Most beginners have a tendency to work too tightly or too loosely, at first. To avoid this, learn to relax your hands and wrists.

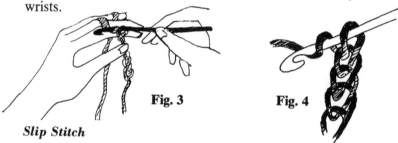

Fig. 3   **Fig. 4**

Slip Stitch

To practice this one, chain 15 or 20 stitches, turn, and with the loop of thread still on the hook, insert it into the center of the first chain stitch that is directly to the left of the hook. Put the thread over the hook, and pull the thread through both loops on the hook. One loop will be on the hook. Repeat until you have worked back to the beginning of the chain.

Single Crochet

Start with 15 or 20 chain stitches, and with the loop of thread still on the hook, insert the hook into the center of the next to last chain stitch. Put the thread over the hook and pull the thread through the first loop on the hook. Put the thread over the hook again and pull the thread through the other loop on the hook. One loop will remain on the hook. Repeat, making a single crochet into each chain stitch until you have reached the beginning of the chain. To continue practicing the single crochet, make 1 chain stitch at the end of the first row of single crochet and turn your work so that the reverse side faces you, and single crochet back to the opposite end. It is customary, when crocheting into a crochet stitch, to insert the hook under the 2 top threads of each stitch.

Double Crochet

Again, chain 20 stitches. Turn. Put the thread over the hook and insert it into the center of the 4th from last chain. Put the thread over the hook again, and draw the hook and thread through the first loop on the hook. Three loops will remain on the hook. Put thread over the hook again, and draw the hook and thread through 2 loops. Two loops will remain on the hook. Put thread over the hook once more, and draw the thread and hook through the 2 remaining loops. There will be 1 loop remaining on the hook. To work the next double crochet, put thread over hook and insert the hook into the next chain stitch.* Repeat from * to * until the row has been completed and each chain has been worked with a double crochet.

Knot Stitch

Attach the thread to the hook and make 1 single crochet. Start the knot stitch by pulling the thread up for ½″, work 1 slip stitch and 1 single crochet, pull the thread up for ½″ and work 1 slip stitch and 1 single crochet. This completes 1 knot stitch. Practice by repeating 10 or 12 times. The slip stitch and the single crochet will form a knot between each ½″ of thread, thus, the knot stitch. These stitches are incorporated into the pattern of the instructions for the beaded necktie in this chapter.

Half Double Crochet

Put thread over the hook and put hook into a single crochet. Put thread over the hook again, and pull the thread through all 3 loops.

Triple Crochet

To make a triple crochet, there must be a loop already on the hook. Put thread over hook, insert the hook into the first stitch to the left, put thread over the hook and draw the thread through this stitch. This will leave 3 loops on the hook. Put thread over the hook, and draw thread through the first 2 loops on the hook. Put thread over the hook once again, and draw the thread through the 2 remaining loops on the hook.

Half Stitch

A half stitch is a slip stitch.

Shell Stitch

The shell stitch is used in 1 pattern only, and is fully described in that project.

Slipping a Bead

Fig. 5 shows the hook passing under the bead and catching the thread on the left side of the bead. Pull the thread through to finish the stitch.

Fig. 5

SINGLE CHAIN NECKLACE

You'll like the pleasant rhythm created by the use of small and large beads in an orderly pattern.

Materials

    No. 4 steel crochet hook
    1 tube tinsel thread, gold or silver
    8 round beads, 8mm size
    63 round beads, 6mm size

Pre-string the beads in the following order: one 8mm, nine 6mm, one 8 mm, nine 6mm, until all of the beads have been strung. Attach the thread to the hook and * chain 15, slip a large bead, chain 15, slip 3 small beads together, chain 8, slip 3 small beads together, chain 8, slip 3 small beads together. Repeat from * until all the beads have been used. Slip-stitch into the 1st chain stitch to join both ends, break the thread, leaving 5 or 6 stitches, and pull it through to secure. Tie the two ends of thread together several times and cut off the excess.

DOUBLE CHAIN NECKLACE

Materials

No. 4 steel crochet hook
1 tube tinsel thread, gold or silver
32 round beads 6mm size (pearl, faceted-plastic moonstones or jeweled)

This chain necklace is approximately 88 inches long and is meant to wrap twice around the neck, making a double strand.

Pre-string 32 beads to the tinsel thread, attach thread to hook and chain 12, * slip a bead, chain 12, slip a bead, chain 12, slip a bead, chain 12, slip a bead, chain 36. Repeat from * until all 32 beads

have been used. Chain 24, slip-stitch into the opposite end of the rope, break the thread, leaving 6 or 7", and pull it through. Tie together the open ends of the threads to secure, and cut away the excess.

A single strand necklace can be made by working only half of the pattern and joining together in the same way.

DANGLE BRACELET

Because this bracelet is made on elastic thread it can be stretched to wear as an anklet also.

Materials

1½ yards of gold elastic thread
9 pearl teardrops or colored plastic-faceted
No. 0 steel crochet hook

Pre-string 7 teardrops to the elastic thread. Chain 9, slip-stitch a bead, chain 9, slip-stitch a bead, etc. until all 7 beads have been used, each one separated by 9 chain stitches. Cut the thread, leaving 4". Slip-stitch into the first chain and pull the thread through to secure. Tie both end threads twice tightly. To the end of each thread, tie on 1 teardrop 1½" from the chain, touch lightly with clear nail polish to secure and cut away excess threads when dry.

DOME RING

Several years ago a dear friend presented me with a ring in this pattern. Since then I have seen it worn by women all over the country. Make it in a color to match your favorite summer frock to give added importance.

Materials

Gold or silver metallic elastic thread
15 plastic, pearl or jeweled beads, 8mm
No. 1 steel crochet hook

Pre-string 15 beads onto the thread. Chain 3, slip-stitch and put the hook into the 1st chain. Slip a bead and complete the stitch. Continue all the way around until the 15 beads have been used. Chain 10 stitches and connect to the opposite side with a slip stitch. Make 1 single crochet into each chain stitch. Slip-stitch, break the thread and pull it through to secure. Leave enough thread to weave in and out to prevent it from ripping apart.

CROCHETED BRACELET WITH BEADS

A wider 4-bead bracelet can be made by increasing the chain to 9, following the same pattern and using 4 beads to each even-numbered row.

Materials

1 ball gold metallic elastic thread
66 plastic-faceted or pearl beads, 8mm
No. 1 steel crochet hook

Row 1: Pre-string 66 beads onto the elastic thread. Chain 7, half stitch into the chain and turn. Consider this row 1.
Row 2: Half stitch into the 1st stitch, slip a bead into the 2nd stitch, half stitch into the 3rd chain, slip a bead into the fourth stitch, etc., to the end of the row. End with a half stitch and turn.
Row 3: Seven half stitches.
Row 4: Repeat row 2. Continue alternating rows 2 and 3 until all the beads have been used. Break thread at the completion of the last row, leaving 12″ of thread. Using the 12″ of thread and a large-eye needle, sew the ends together.

CLEOPATRA SANDALS No. 1

Boutiques would charge fat-cat fees for sandals like these, but you can raid your lean-cat sugarbowl and buy the makings. Orange and brown, I think, make an appealing combination, but you might have other ideas.

Materials

1 spool orange macramé nylon cord
No. 5 (F) plastic crochet hook
14 brown wooden beads, 12mm or 18mm size

Attach the nylon cord to the needle and chain 80, leaving approximately 8″ of cord at each end. Put a large bead onto each 8″ length and a knot at the end. Use a small amount of Elmer's Glue to keep the open end of the cord from fraying, then tie another knot on the opposite side of the bead to hold it in place.

Cut 3 pieces of cord 5½″ long and knot one end of each. To the unknotted end of each, transfer one large wooden bead. For the right sandal, find the center of the chain by folding it in half. Six stitches from the center, on both sides, join the chains with one of the 5½″ lengths of cord by tying it around both chains. Leave ¾″ so that the bead will dangle. To the chain on the right side, count 10 chain stitches and insert the open end of another 5½″ length of cord into the center of the chain stitch. Put a bead on the open end and knot the end of the cord. Count back 10 more stitches, and add the 3rd ball in the same way. Repeat for the left sandal, but add the beads to the left side of the chain.

To wear, insert the big toe, from back to front, into the loop. Wrap each end around the ankle, first to the back, then to the front, and fasten by tying the two ends together at the front of the ankle.

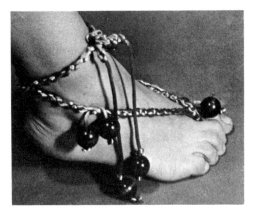 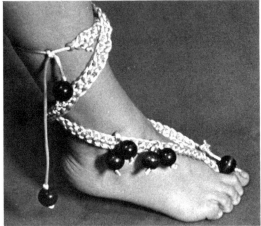

CLEOPATRA SANDALS No. 2

The only difference between the preceding pattern and this one is the width of the straps. No. 2 has a row of single crochet added to the chain except for the section that goes under the big toe.

Materials

1 spool yellow nylon macramé cord
No. 5 (F) plastic crochet hook
14 brown wooden beads, 12mm or 18mm size

Chain 98. For the next row, single crochet for 49 stitches, chain 12, slip-stitch into the first chain, then single crochet to the remaining 49 chains. Add the wooden balls the same as for pattern No. 1.

CHIGNON SNOOD

Materials

1 tube gold elastic thread
No. 4 steel crochet hook
30 beads, 6mm size

Put 30 beads on the thread and Chain 6 and join to form a ring. Chain 3, make 12 double crochets in the ring and join to the top of Chain 3.

Row 1: Work 3 double crochets in the same stitch of chain 3. In the second double crochet slip-stitch a bead. Chain 2, skip a chain and double crochet 3 in the next stitch. Again slip-stitch a bead into the 2nd double crochet. Chain 2, skip a chain, etc. all the way around and join in the top of chain 3.

Row 2: * Double crochet 1 in the chain 3 stitch. Chain 2, work 2 double crochets in the same stitch. This will equal 1 shell stitch. Chain 2, work 1 shell stitch in the chain 2 space. Repeat from * all the way around and join in the top of chain 3.

Row 3: * Work 1 shell in the first shell. In the chain 2 of this first shell slip-stitch a bead. Chain 2 and work 1 shell in the next shell, slip-stitch a bead in the chain 2 of the 2nd shell. Repeat from * all the way around and join in chain 3.

Row 4: Repeat row 2.

Row 5: Repeat row 3.

Row 6: Chain 6, single crochet in the 1st shell, slip-stitch a bead, chain 6, single crochet in the next shell, slip-stitch a bead, chain 6, single crochet in the next shell, etc. all the way around and join in the 3rd stitch of the chain 6.

Rows 7 through 12: Chain 6, single crochet into the 1st loop of chain 6. Chain 6, single crochet into the 2nd loop. Chain 6, single crochet into the 3rd loop and repeat all the way around. At the completion of the 12th row, fasten, break the thread and pull it through to secure.

Drawstring

Chain 115, leaving a 6″ piece of thread on each end. Thread 4 beads on one end close to the last chain and knot the end close to the beads. Repeat on the other end. Thread the chain through the openings of the 12th row, over and under, all the way around. Pull the drawstrings under the chignon and tie to secure.

BLUE, AQUA AND GOLD ROPE BELT

Materials

290 dark blue oat moonstones
290 aqua oat moonstones
586 small gold beads, 2mm or 2½mm size
2 large filigree caps
2 head pins
2 small jump rings
1 large jump ring
1 large spring ring
No. 10 crochet hook
No. 30 crochet thread

Onto a ball of crochet thread, * string 1 light bead, 1 dark bead, 1 light, 1 dark for 20 beads (10 of each color), then 12 small gold beads. Repeat from * until all beads have been strung.

Attach crochet hook to thread and chain 5. Join into the 1st chain with a slip-stitch to form a ring. Slip a bead, and single crochet into the center of the ring, continuing for 4 beads. Slip a 5th bead, put the hook into the thread at the bottom of the 1st bead, and single crochet. Slip another bead, and single crochet into the bottom threads of the 2nd bead, etc., around and around. You will be matching the color of the bead to the one you will be working into. When you come to the 12 small gold beads, treat 3 gold beads as 1 bead for 4 times, and continue until all beads have been used. Break the thread, leaving about 8″, and pull it through to secure. Tie a head pin to each end, knotting each one 3 times and securing with adhesive. Cut away excess thread when dry. Add a large filigree cap to each end, trim away ½″ of the pin and ring the end closed with pliers.

Tassel

With a fine beading needle, make 5 strands of 25 beads each, using the small gold beads. At the end of each strand, bypass the bottom bead, and bring the needle and thread up through the remaining 24 beads. Tie all top threads together, once, by dividing them in half (5 on one side and 5 on the other). Insert a head pin into the second knot, apply adhesive to the threads, pull the knot closed and knot once more. Trim off the excess threads when dry. Put a medium-sized filigree cap onto the head pin, snip off ½″, insert it into the ringed head pin at one end of the crocheted belt, and ring the head pin closed. Make another tassel for the other end, and attach. To close the belt, a large jump ring has been attached to one side of the belt, and a large spring ring to the opposite side. Attach these to fit your waistline.

BLUE, AQUA AND GOLD ROPE BRACELET

Materials

    64 dark blue oat moonstones
    64 aqua oat moonstones
    132 small gold beads, 2mm or 2½mm size
    2 large gold filigree caps
    1 small gold filigree cap
    1 small spring ring
    2 large jump rings
    3 gold head pins

Transfer all the beads to the ball of thread following the same sequence as for the belt. Attach a head pin and a large filigree cap to each end. To one end attach a large jump ring. To the other end, attach a small spring ring.

Tassel

Make the tassel the same as the belt, but use 12 beads for each of the 5 strands. Bypass the bottom bead on each strand, and bring needle and thread up through the remaining 11 beads. Tie all threads together at the top, tie on a head pin, securing the knots with adhesive. Cut away excess threads when dry. Add a small filigree cap to the head pin, cut away all but ½" of the pin, and ring it through a large jump ring. Attach the large jump ring to the other jump ring at one end of the bracelet.

BEADED NECKTIE

Materials

1 ball Bucilla silver brocade thread
No. 4 steel crochet hook
118 aqua moonstones or pearls, 6mm size

Tie

Pre-string approximately 96 beads onto the ball of thread and attach the thread to the hook. Work 1 single crochet, then 15 knot stitches. Turn your work. Make 1 knot stitch and single crochet into the first knot of the knot stitch to the left of the hook. Slip a bead with a slip stitch. Make 1 knot stitch into the knot of the 2nd knot stitch, slip a bead with a slip stitch and continue in this manner to the end of the row, slipping a bead with a slip stitch into each knot as you work. Turn, and repeat, until you have 7 rows in all. Single crochet 1 row across the bottom. Cut thread and pull through the last stitch to secure.

Top Band

Pre-string 22 beads onto the ball of thread.
Row 1: Attach the thread to the hook and chain 9. Slip a bead with a slip stitch and make 1 single crochet. Slip a bead with a slip stitch and make 1 single crochet, etc., until 11 beads have been added.
Row 2: Slip-stitch into the 1st chain to the left of the hook and single crochet without beads across the row. Slip-stitch and turn your work.
Rows, 3, 4, 5 and 6: Repeat as for row 2 ending each row with a slip stitch.
Row 7: Turn and single crochet for 9 stitches. Slip a bead with a

slip stitch into each of the next 11 single crochets and single crochet for 9 stitches to the end of Row 7. Break the thread and pull it through to secure. Join the two ends together by slip-stitching.

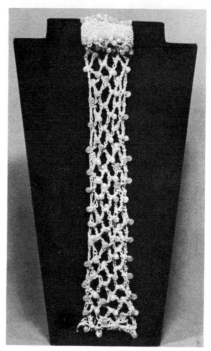

Tie String

Transfer 3 beads to the ball of thread and attach the thread to the hook. Chain 1 and slip a bead. Chain 6, working the tag end of the thread into the chain. Slip a bead, chain 6, slip a bead and chain 30. Slip-stitch into the upper right side of the top bead, break thread and pull it through to secure. Put a needle on the remaining thread and sew the tie string to the tie band. Repeat for the opposite side. Sew the top of the side to the bottom of the tie band, directly under the row of 11 beads.

BEADED EYEGLASS CASE

Glamour for glasses? Why not; when it takes only minutes of your time and not too much money. Pearls complement the gray and silver threads of the background, and make your eyeglass case pretty and always easy to find.

Materials

1 ball of Knit-Cro-Sheen in gray
1 tube of single ply silver tinsel thread
No. 4 steel crochet hook
60 pearls, 5 or 6mm size

Front

Pre-string the 60 beads onto the ball of Knit Cro-Sheen, and attach both threads to the crochet hook, working with the 2 colors simultaneously.

Chain 21 and turn. Single crochet into the 2nd chain from the hook. This forms the 1st stitch. Continue to single crochet all the way across (20 in all). Turn.

Row 1: Chain 2 and double crochet in each single crochet and turn.

Row 2: Chain 1, single crochet into the 2nd double crochet of the 1st row, slip a bead, make 1 single crochet into each of the next 2 stitches, slip a bead, etc., to the end of the row, and turn. You will have used 9 beads for the 20 stitches.

Row 3: Chain 2, double crochet into the last single crochet of Row 2, double crochet into each single crochet to the end of the row and turn.

Row 4: Chain 1, single crochet into the last 4 single crochets of the 3rd row. Slip a bead, 4 single crochets, slip a bead, etc., to the end of the row, and turn.

Repeat rows 3 and 4, alternately, for approximately 5".

Decrease 2 stitches on 1 side of the last double crochet row for the next 4 rows, following the pattern.

Last row: Single crochet on the last 12 stitches, break the thread, and pull it through to fasten.

Back

The back is worked the same as the front, but without beads, and with no decreases.

When the back measures the same as the front, don't break the thread, but join both pieces together, right sides out, and single crochet all around the 3 sides, leaving the top open. At the 2 bottom corners, work 2 single crochets. This will make a neater corner.

CROCHETED NECKTIE WITH PEARLS

Sparkle up that dark dress or shift with this flattering pearl-crusted crocheted necktie—today's version of the classic string of pearls.

Materials

No. 4 steel crochet hook
2 tubes of silver tinsel thread
135 pearls (approximately), 6 mm size

Pre-string the pearls to the tube of silver thread and attach the thread to the hook. For this pattern, you will start at the top.

Row 1: Chain 21 and turn.

Row 2: Single crochet into each chain, picking up the back half of the stitch only, and turn.

Row 3: Single crochet 2, slip-stitch a bead, single crochet 4, slip-stitch a bead, single crochet 4, slip-stitch a bead, single crochet 4, slip-stitch a bead, single crochet 4, slip-stitch a bead, single crochet 2, and turn.

Rows 4, 5 and 6: These 3 rows are single crochet, into the back half of the stitch only.

Row 7: Single crochet 3, slip-stitch a bead, single crochet 5, slip-stitch a bead, single crochet 5, slip-stitch a bead, single crochet 5, slip-stitch a bead, single crochet 2 and turn.

Rows 8, 9 and 10: Repeat Rows 4, 5 and 6.

Row 11: Repeat Row 3.

Rows 12, 13 and 14: Repeat Rows 4, 5 and 6.

Row 15: Repeat Row 7.

Rows 16, 17 and 18: Repeat Rows 4, 5 and 6.

Repeat from Row 3 through row 18 until the entire tie measures approximately 10″.

Starting the decrease

Decrease 1 stitch on each side, then at the beginning and end of every 2nd row, decrease 1 stitch, keeping the pattern until 2 stitches remain. While decreasing, in order to keep the pattern of Row 7, add 1 pearl at the end of the row if 4 stitches instead of 5 stitches should remain. When there are 2 stitches left, slip-stitch these last 2 stitches together to make the point at the bottom of the tie, break the thread and pull it through to secure.

Back Band and Top of Tie

Attach thread to the right side of the front and chain 10. Attach to the left side. Single crochet in the 20 stitches at the top of the tie, with the wrong side facing you. Continue with single crochet into the next 10 chains, with the right side facing you. For the next 10 rows, working only the front of the tie, keep the pattern of the beads by slipping a bead into every 2nd stitch on every other row. The rows in between are single crochet. At the same time, decrease 1 stitch on each side until 9 stitches are left.

Work the pearl pattern with the wrong side facing you, and the single crochets with the right side facing.

At the completion of the last row, leave the thread attached, chain

40 and single crochet the chain. Break the thread and pull it through to secure. Attach the ball thread to the opposite side of the tie and repeat the chain of 40, then single crochet back. This will enable you to tie the two ends together under the collar of a blouse or shirt.

BEADED COLLAR WITH PEARLS

Complement a simple dress and give it a lift with this soft and flattering beaded collar. It is stunning worked in black with gold beads or metallic thread and pearls.

Materials

1 ball of Knit-Cro-Sheen, any color
208 pearls, 3mm or 4mm size
No. 7 steel crochet hook

Pre-string 208 pearls to the ball of thread. Starting at the neck edge, chain 2½" longer than neck measurement. Eight chain stitches should be equal to 1".

Row 1: Double crochet into the 4th chain from the hook. Double crochet into each chain across for the desired length. Chain 3 and turn.

Row 2: Skip the first double crochet and double crochet into each double crochet across making sure to put hook into the top of the turning chain. Chain 3 and turn.

Row 3: Skip the first double crochet and double crochet into the next double crochet. Slide a bead close to the hook and make another double crochet in the same place as the last double crochet. * Skip the next double crochet. Double crochet in the next double crochet, slide a bead close to the hook and double crochet in the same place as the last double crochet. Repeat from * all the way across and into the next turning chain. Double crochet into the top of the turning chain. Chain 3 and turn.

Row 4: Skip the 1st double crochet, make 2 double crochets in the next double crochet. * Chain 1, skip the next double crochet. Work 2 double crochets in the next double crochet. Repeat from * all the way across. Skip the next double crochet in the top of the turning chain. Chain 3 and turn.

Row 5: Skip the first double crochet and double crochet into the next double crochet. Slide a bead close to the hook and double crochet in the same place as the last double crochet. * Chain 1, skip the next double crochet. Double crochet into the next double crochet, slide a bead close to the hook and double crochet in the same place as the last double crochet. Repeat from * all the way across and double crochet in the top of the turning chain. Chain 3 and turn.

Row 6: * Skip the next double crochet, work 2 double crochets in the next double crochet. Repeat from * all the way across, double crochet in the top of the turning chain. Chain 3 and turn.

Row 7: Repeat the 5th row but substitute 2 chains instead of 1 chain. Chain 3 and turn.

Row 8: Repeat the 6th row, chain 3 and turn.

Row 9: Repeat the 7th row. Break the thread and pull through to secure. The beading is completed, so remove any remaining beads from the ball of thread.

Edging

With the right side of your work facing you, and along one narrow edge, attach the thread to the top of the end stitch of the 2nd row. Chain 1 over the first stitch of the 2nd row. * Single crochet, chain 2 and work 4 double crochets in the first loop. This will complete 1 shell stitch. Repeat from * to the end. Skip the 1st stitch of the next row. Make a shell stitch into each space of the preceding row until 3 shell stitches have been made. This will bring you to the bottom edge of the collar. Working along the outer edge, make a shell stitch in each of the chain-2-spaces all the way across to the next corner. Work another narrow edge to correspond with the opposite narrow edge. Break the thread and pull through to secure.

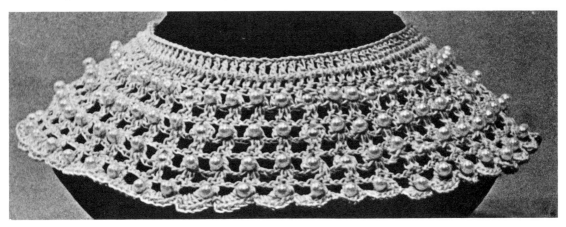

SACHET BAG

Add a touch of charm to your clothes or storage closet and at the same time keep it fresh and sweetly scented. The bag can be filled with cloves, dried rose petals, lavender or your favorite sachet. Use any coordinating colors you like, of course.

Materials

1 ball of Knit-Cro-Sheen thread in yellow
1 ball of Knit Cro-Sheen thread in green
75 orange plastic-faceted beads, 8mm size
30 green plastic-faceted beads, 6mm size
No. 5 steel crochet hook

Bag

Transfer approximately 75 orange beads to the ball of yellow thread and chain 2. As you work the following pattern, slip-stitch a bead on every 3rd round.

Round 1: Work 5 single crochet into the 2nd chain from the hook. Do not join the rounds. Attach a small safety pin to the last stitch and this will indicate the beginning of the rounds.

Round 2: Work 2 single crochets in each single crochet around for 10 stitches.

Round 3: * Start adding beads on this round and work 2 single crochets in the next single crochet. Repeat from * all the way around. This will be 5 single crochets increased.

Round 4: Increase 5 single crochets, evenly spaced, single crochet into each single crochet. Repeat until there are 64 single crochets on the round. Make sure the increases do not overlap the increases of the previous round.

Round 5: Single crochet in each single crochet around. Repeat this round until the length from the center measures about 4″. Remember to add beads every 3rd round.

Last round: * Single crochet in the next single crochet. Chain 5 and skip the next single crochet. Repeat from * all the way around. Join with a slip stitch to the next single crochet, break thread and pull it through to secure.

Cord

Using a double thread of green, make a chain 16″ long. Break the thread and pull it through to secure. Draw the chain through the loops of the last round of the bag.

Leaf

Make 6 leaves in green on single thread.

Transfer the 30 green beads to the thread and chain 17.

First row: Single crochet in the 2nd chain from the hook. Single crochet in the next 2 single crochets, half double crochet in the next chain, double crochet in the next chain, triple crochet in the next 6 chains, double crochet in the next chain, half double crochet in the next chain, single crochet in the next 2 single crochets in the last chain.

Working along the opposite side of the starting chain, single crochet in the next 2 chains, half double crochet in the next chain, double crochet in the next chain, triple crochet in the next 6 chains, double crochet in the next chain, half double crochet in the next chain, single crochet in the next 2 chains, and single crochet in the same place where the first single crochet was made. Turn.

Second row: Slip-stitch in the first 5 stitches, slip-stitch a bead in the 6th stitch. Slip-stitch for 5 stitches, slip-stitch a bead in the 12th stitch. Slip-stitch for 5 stitches and slip a bead. Slip-stitch in each stitch all the way around, adding a bead to the 6th, 12th, 18th, 24th and 30th stitches. Slip-stitch to the end. Break the thread and pull it through to secure. Fill the sachet bag, pull the cord tightly, knot it and make a bow. Sew a leaf to each end of the cord and sew the remaining 4 leaves to the top of the bag.

BATHROOM TISSUE COVER

This bit of glamour for the bathroom is made with two contrasting colors. Make it in one color if you choose, but use double thread. *Color Plate No. I* shows pink and blue.

Materials

> 2 balls Knit-Cro-Sheen thread, one each of any two colors
> 70 faceted beads, 6mm size
> No. 4 steel crochet hook

Working with 2 threads, transfer 40 beads to the double thread, chain 6 and slip-stitch into the 1st chain to form a ring.

Round 2: Work 12 double crochets into the ring.

Round 3: Working round, chain 5, double crochet into the next stitch, chain 1, double crochet into the next stitch and repeat to the end of the round. Slip-stitch into the 4th stitch of the first chain.

Round 4: Slip-stitch into the 4th stitch of the first chain. Chain 5, double crochet into the 1st chain, chain 2, double crochet in the next space, chain 2, double crochet in the next stitch and repeat to the end of the round, slip-stitching into the 4th stitch of the first chain.

Round 5: Chain 5, double crochet in the 1st stitch, chain 3, double crochet in the next stitch and repeat to the end of the round, slip-stitching into the 4th stitch of the first chain.

Round 6: Repeat round 5.

Round 7: Chain 5, double crochet 3 in the next stitch, chain 2, double crochet 3 in the next space and repeat to the end of the round. Slip-stitch into the 4th stitch of the first chain.

Round 8: Repeat round 7.

Round 9: Single crochet into each stitch around and the 2 single crochets between the double crochets. Slip-stitch into the 4th stitch of the first chain.

Round 10: Chain 5, double crochet in 3rd chain, chain 2, double crochet in 3rd chain, skip 2 chains, then double crochet in 3rd chain. Continue all the way around and slip-stitch into the 4th stitch of the first chain.

Round 11: Chain 5, double crochet 2 in the next space, chain 2, double crochet in the next space, chain 2, double crochet 2 in the next space, chain 2, double crochet in the next space and repeat all the way around, slip-stitch into the 4th stitch of the first chain.

Round 12: Repeat round 10.

Round 13: Repeat round 11.

Round 14: Repeat round 10 with 1 single crochet between each double crochet instead of 2 double crochets.

Round 15: Repeat round 11 with 1 chain between each double crochet instead of 2 single crochets.

Round 16: Repeat round 14.

Round 17: Shell stitch.

Chain 5, slip-stitch a bead, * Double crochet 2 in the same space, 2 single crochet and 3 double crochet in the same space with a bead slip-stitched in the 2nd double crochet. Chain 1 in the next space, double crochet 3 in the next space with a bead slip-stitched in the 2nd double crochet. Chain 2, double crochet 3 in the same space with a bead slip-stitched in the 2nd double crochet. Repeat from * all the way around.

Last row: Single crochet in each single stitch. In the top of each shell, single crochet 2, slip-stitch a bead and single crochet in the same space. Single crochet in each single crochet to the next shell stitch and in top of each shell, single crochet 2, slip-stitch a bead and single crochet in the same space. Repeat from * all the way around. Break the thread and pull through to secure.

Top Tassel

Transfer 30 beads onto double thread. Chain 4 and slip-stitch a bead, chain 4 and slip-stitch a bead until 15 beads have been used, then turn. Chain 3, slip-stitch a bead in a single crochet and single crochet into the stitch of the last bead. Chain 3, slip-stitch a bead and single crochet into the next bead stitch. Work to the end of the row, slip-stitch a bead into the last stitch. Slip-stitch into the first stitch, break thread and pull through to secure. Fold the tassel in half and tie to the top of the cover.

Crocheted Circles

There really is no limit to what can be created with plastic curtain rings, a crochet hook and various threads. On the following pages are just a few uses, and if it looks familiar to you, it's because each ring strangely resembles the pulls that have been used for years on window shades. Perhaps these designs will inspire you to find new ideas of your own. The basic method will be explained here so that it won't have to be repeated with each set of instructions.

Attach the thread to the crochet hook in the usual way and set a ring on top of the thread, close to the hook. * Insert the hook into the center of the ring, bring the thread over the hook and bring the thread and the hook back up through the center of the ring. Bring the thread over the hook and draw the thread through the 1st thread on the hook. Bring the thread over the hook once again and draw the thread and hook through both threads on the hook. Repeat from * until the entire ring is covered. The stitches should rest on the outer rim of the ring. Keep the threads close together. At the completion of the last stitch, slip-stitch into the first stitch, break the thread and pull it through to secure.

For a wider ridge of stitches, work a row of single crochet on the top of the ring after each yarn over. Once the ring is covered, any number of stitches can be added to embellish the circle; double crochet, shell stitch, etc. slipping a bead or two into the pattern as you work.

RED, WHITE AND BLUE BELT WITH LARGE RINGS

Geometric designs can have a soft look. I especially like the comfort and flexibility of this belt. It's easy to scale down, too, if you like it narrower.

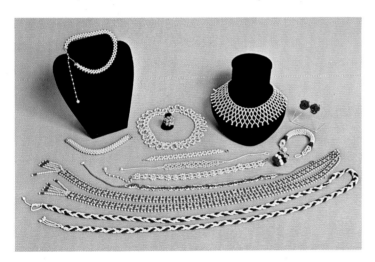

I. Collar, p. 26; snood, p. 17; Change purse, p. 45; bathroom tissue cover, p. 30; necktie, p. 24; eyeglass case, p. 22; silver belt and earrings, p. 38, belt, earrings, p. 32.

II. Choker, p. 70; bracelet, p. 68; necklace and ring, p. 59; bib, p. 60; earrings, p. 126; bracelet, p. 50; chokers, p.52; headband, p. 54; dome ring, p. 15; bracelet, p. 65; pearl belt, p. 79; braided belt (see rope belt), p. 81.

III. Moroccan necklace, earrings and bracelet, p. 71; scarf necklaces, p. 51; evening bag, p. 77; teardrop earrings and necklace, p. 63; braided belt, p. 81.

IV. Swag necklace, p. 88; bracelet, p. 87; Sputnik earrings, p. 95; six chain necklaces, p. 89-92; choker, p. 96; dangle earrings, necklace, p. 95.

V. Jacket, p. 117; daisy belt, p. 123; choker, p. 119; necklace and earrings, p. 120; orange blossom necklace, p. 123; daisy necklace, p. 121.

VI. Arrangement, 22" high, 14½" wide, with snapdragons, p. 158; columbines, p. 153; black-eyed Susans, p. 151.

Materials

1 skein each red, white, and blue, 3-ply, wool yarn
167 white faceted plastic beads, 6mm
81 blue faceted plastic beads, 6mm
162 red faceted plastic beads 6mm
14 plastic curtain rings, 1½″ in diameter
4 plastic curtain rings, ½″ in diameter
No. 5 (F) plastic crochet hook
No. 4 steel crochet hook

Although this belt is shown with 3 red, 6 white, and 5 blue rings, any combination of 2 or 3 colors can be used for this bold accessory to a pants suit or basic dress. It is also most attractive in a solid color with contrasting beads. Fourteen rings are sufficient for a size 12 waist.

Working with the white yarn and the blue beads, transfer at least 27 beads to the yarn. Use a large-eye needle for stringing, or dip the end of the yarn into a bit of Elmer's Glue, twist the yarn threads together to tighten the strands. Let dry for a minute or two and the stiffened end will work like a needle for stringing the beads.

Attach the No. 5 plastic hook to the yarn and cover the ring with 54 single crochet stitches. Change to the No. 4 steel hook and, without turning the ring, work 2 single crochet stitches, slip a bead, 2 single crochets, slip a bead, etc., all the way around. Slip-stitch, break the thread and pull it through the stitch to secure. Make 5 more rings in white—6 in all.

Cover 5 rings with blue wool and white beads, and 3 with red wool and blue beads.

Make 4 blue rings in the smaller size and trim them with white beads. Use 8 white beads for each ring with 2 single crochets between each bead.

Ties, and Assembling Rings

There are 2 tie ends, each consisting of a chain of 54 plus 1 row of single crochet.

Using the extended pieces of yarn on each ring, sew the rings together, lengthwise; 1 red, 2 white, 2 blue, 1 red, 2 white, 2 blue, 1 red, 2 white, 1 blue. Sew a tie to each end and at the bottom of each tie, sew on the 2 smaller rings that have been sewn together.

BLUE AND WHITE RING EARRINGS

Try this same design using gold or silver threads and 6mm pearls for a dressier effect.

BLUE AND WHITE RING EARRINGS

Materials

No. 4 steel hook
2 earring backs with perforated discs
30 white faceted beads, 6mm
2 plastic curtain rings, ⅝" in diameter
blue 3-ply wool yarn

Fig. 6

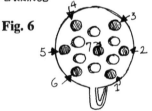

Pre-string 8 white beads to the blue yarn. Cover a ⅝" plastic ring with 16 single crochets. For the 2nd row, without turning the ring, slip a bead with a slip stitch, 2 single crochet, slip a bead, 2 single crochets all the way around the ring. Chain 8. Allow 15" of yarn, break the thread and pull it through to secure. Tie the ring tightly to the base of the earring back and add a needle to the 15" of yarn. Bring needle from the back, into hole No. 1. *Fig. 6.* Put on a bead, bring needle down through hole No. 2, bring needle up through hole No. 3, put on a bead, bring needle down through No. 2, up through No. 4, put on a bead, down through No. 3, up through No. 5, put on a bead, down through No. 4, up through No. 6, put on a bead, down through No. 5, up through No. 1, put on a bead and back down through No. 6, up through the center hole, put on a bead and back down No. 6.

Sew through the stitches on the back of the disc several times to secure, and cut off excess thread. Repeat for the other earring.

SQUARE BELT WITH PEARL TEARDROPS

Materials

1 ball Bucilla gold brocade
24 plastic squares
24 pearl teardrops
No. 4 steel crochet hook

Because curtain rings aren't square, use your ingenuity and create a form for this belt. Duplicate the printed pattern shown, in cardboard for easier tracing, and cut 24 squares from the lids, sides and bottoms of any lightweight plastic containers. Margarine tubs are excellent, for instance.

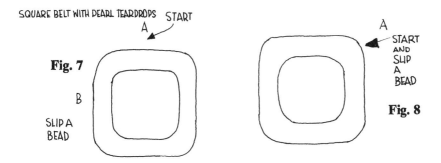

Making the Squares

Transfer 24 pearl teardrops to the ball of thread, and attach the thread to the hook. Starting in the middle of 1 side of a square, in *Fig. 7 (A)*, work a single crochet around the square to the middle of the 2nd side, in *Fig. 7 (B)*, slip-stitch a bead, and cover the rest of the square. Slip-stitch into the 1st single crochet to join, break thread, leaving 10″, and pull the thread through to secure. Cover 22 in all. On the 2 remaining squares, start the thread on 1 corner, in *Fig. 8 (A),* work 1 single crochet, slip-stitch a bead into the corner and then work all the way around. These 2 squares will be used at the ends of the ties on either side of the belt.

Assembling the Squares

Using the extended threads on the squares and a large-eyed embroidery needle, sew together 22 squares so that the teardrops hang from the centers of the top sides.

Tie

Attach the ball of thread to the hook and slip-stitch into the lower corner of the end square. Chain 52 and attach it to the top corner of one of the squares that has the pearl in the corner. Work a single crochet back up the chain for 46 stitches. Chain 6 and attach it to the top corner of the end square. Repeat for the other end of the belt. To close the belt, put 1 end square through the 2 chain sections in the opposite end of the belt and tie both ends together. ,

GREEN TRIANGLE BELT

So very pretty, you'll be choosing your pants suit or dress to complement the belt instead of the other way around! It would be equally effective in go-with-everything neutral colors or gold and silver thread.

Materials

    Green Bucilla brocade
    22 triangles cut from plastic containers   **Fig. 9**
    No. 4 steel crochet hook
    22 gold teardrops

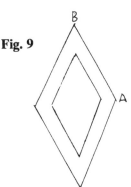

Using the printed pattern, duplicate it in cardboard, then trace and cut 22 triangles from the sides and lids of any soft plastic containers. Transfer 22 gold teardrops to the spool of yarn and cover all of them in the usual manner (single crochet). However, this time slip a teardrop into the top point of 20 of the triangles, *Fig. 9 (A),* and on the 2 remaining triangles, slip a teardrop at *(B).* These last triangles will be attached at the end of the ties of 70 chain stitches and 1 row of single crochet. Sew together the 20 triangles, and add a tie string to each end.

TRIANGLE EARRINGS

Bangles, not to jangle, but to fall softly to frame the face. Choose lightweight teardrops if you don't like the feel of a heavy earring.

Materials

2 plastic triangles
2 gold teardrops
green Bucilla brocade
2 earring backs with ear cups
2 gold (round) beads, 8mm
No. 4 steel crochet hook

Cut out and cover 2 more triangles, adding the teardrops. *Fig. 9 (B).* Glue an 8mm round gold bead into the cup of each earring back and tie a triangle to each.

SILVER CIRCLE BELT

Materials

44 plastic curtain rings ⅞" in diameter
2 balls Bucilla silver brocade
No. 4 steel crochet hook

The materials have been planned for an average size 12 waistline. Each ring, when completed, will measure about 1¼" in diameter.

Attach the end of the thread to the hook. Set one ring on the tip of the thread, close to the hook. Insert the hook into the center of the plastic ring, yarn over hook and pull the thread up through the center of the ring. Work 1 single crochet on the top edge of the ring. Insert the hook into the center of the ring again, yarn over hook, pull the thread up through the center of the ring. Work another single crochet on the top edge of the ring. Continue in this manner until the plastic ring is covered—about 25 stitches. Slip-stitch into the 1st single crochet to join, break thread, leaving about 10" and pull the thread through to secure. Make 44 rings in all for the belt and the tie ends.

Using the 10" of thread that has been left on each circle, sew together 2 separate strips of 20 circles each, then sew the 2 strips together, side by side. Sew 1 circle to each end, between the 2 end circles. To the bottom of the end circle on each side, slip-stitch the ball thread, and chain 90. Slip-stitch into another crocheted circle at the point where the end thread was left. Cut off all but 4″ of the extended length of thread on the circle, single crochet back for the full length of the chain (90 stitches), and include the 4″ of thread as you work the single crochet. At the completion of the row of single crochet, slip-stitch once more into the bottom ring of the belt, break the thread and pull through to secure.

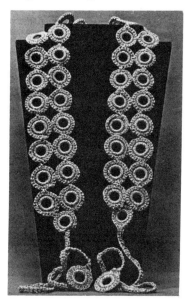

SILVER CIRCLE EARRINGS

Materials

    2 beads, silver or pearl, 8mm
    2 earring backs with cups
    No. 4 steel crochet hook
    2 plastic curtain rings, ½″
    2 curtain rings ⅝″ in diameter
    2 curtain rings ⅞″ in diameter
    Bucilla silver brocade

Cover ½ of the smallest ring with single crochet as described in instructions for silver ring belt—about 8 stitches. Join one ⅝″ ring with single crochet and cover it half way around. Attach one ⅞″ ring with 1 single crochet, to the bottom of the ⅝″ ring and work all the way around.

Cover the remaining half of the ⅝″ ring and the remaining half of the ½″ ring. Slip-stitch into the 1st single crochet of the smallest ring, break threads and pull it through to secure. Use the ends of the threads to tie the 3 joined circles to the earring back. Glue a silver jeweled or a pearl bead to the cup of the earring back. This completes 1 earring. Repeat to make the pair.

BOLERO JACKET OF CROCHETED CIRCLES

A perfect traveling companion and a glamorous quick change for a basic pants suit or cocktail dress, this gold bolero unpacks without a wrinkle and is lightweight to wear. The materials listed will make a size 8 or 10.

Materials

> 10 balls of Bucilla gold brocade thread
> 248 plastic curtain rings, ⅞″ in diameter
> No. 4 steel crochet hook

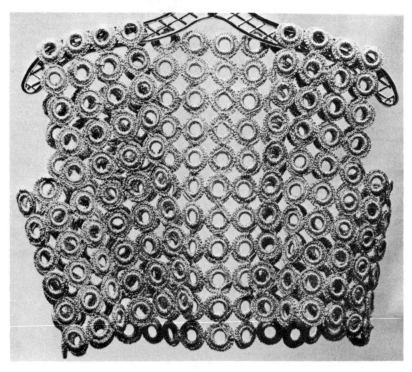

Cover 248 plastic rings as described under *Crocheted Circles* earlier in this chapter. The circles will be sewn together after first making 3 separate sections of the pattern, then combining the 3. Leave 10 or 12″ of thread on each circle for sewing together.

Back

Sew 132 circles together to form a rectangle 12 circles wide and 11 circles long. To both sides of the bottom 6 rows sew on 1 circle. *Fig. 10.*

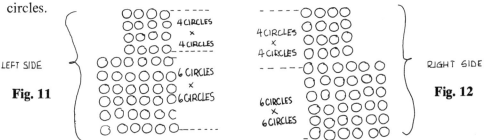

Fig. 10

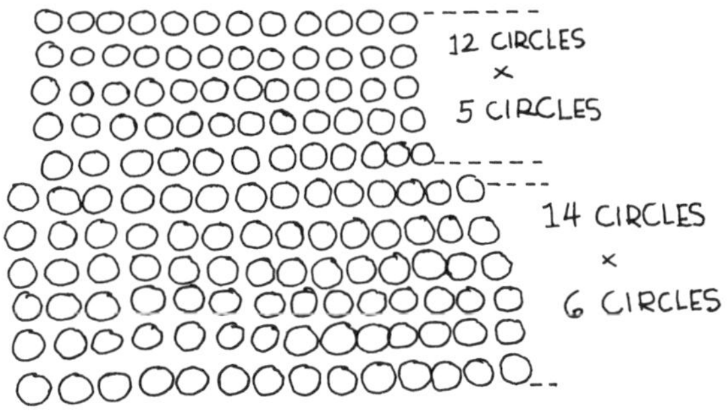

BACK →

12 CIRCLES
×
5 CIRCLES

14 CIRCLES
×
6 CIRCLES

Left Side

Sew 40 circles together to form a rectangle 4 circles wide and 10 circles long. On the left edge of each of the bottom 6 rows sew on 2 circles. *Fig. 11.*

Right Side

Repeat the combination of 40 circles, the same as for the left side, but sew 2 circles to the right side of each of the bottom 6 rows. *Fig. 12.*

Combining Back and Sides

Sew the left front to the left side of the back section, and the right front to the right side of the back section. Connect edges only.

For a size 12, add an extra row of circles on the top of each section. This will drop the armhole. For the extra width, add 1 circle to each side edge of the bottom 6 rows. You will need 32 extra circles.

LEFT SIDE

Fig. 11

4 CIRCLES
×
4 CIRCLES

6 CIRCLES
×
6 CIRCLES

4 CIRCLES
×
4 CIRCLES

6 CIRCLES
×
6 CIRCLES

RIGHT SIDE

Fig. 12

PLACE MATS WITH BEADS

Brown and orange raffia straw was chosen for these, but any combination of colors that blends with china or room decorations will be just as striking.

Materials (for 1 Mat)

> 28 plastic curtain rings, 1½" in diameter
> 12 plastic curtain rings, ⅝" in diameter
> 1 tube orange raffia straw
> 1 tube brown raffia straw
> 36 brown wooden balls, 10mm size
> No. 5 (F) plastic crochet hook

Each ring is covered with the raffia straw as described under *Crocheted Circles* earlier in this chapter. Your work will have fewer joinings if you make 4 strips of 5 rings each in orange and then tie the 4 strips together. Make a row of 5 rings by first covering one half of the 1st ring. At this point, attach and cover the 2nd ring halfway. Add the 3rd and 4th in the same way, working only halfway around each ring after it has been attached. *Fig. 13.* Attach the 5th ring and work all the way around, then cover the other half of the 4th, 3rd, 2nd and 1st rings. Tie together the 4 strips of 5 rings each with short pieces of the raffia straw, knotting the raffia 3 or 4 times, securely, on the wrong side of your work. Add just a touch of clear nail polish to each knot for added security and cut off the excess pieces of raffia when dry.

To work the 2 strips of 4 rings each in brown, pre-string 24 of the wooden balls to the brown raffia. Working each ring individually, cover a ring with 16 stitches, slip a bead, make 2 stitches into the ring, slip a bead, make 2 stitches into the ring, slip a bead and continue around the ring with 16 more stitches to cover. *Fig. 14.* Slip-stitch into the 1st stitch of the ring, break the thread, and pull the raffia through to secure. The 2 ends of the thread will be used to tie the brown rings to the orange ones. Make 8 beaded rings in brown. Tie together 2 strips of 4 rings each, then tie a strip to each end of the combined orange rings.

42

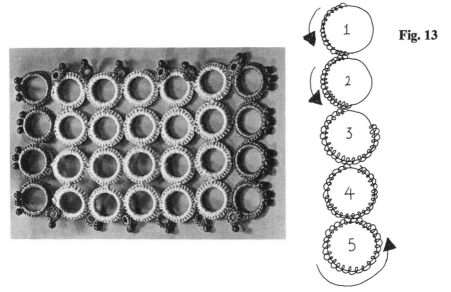

Fig. 13

Smaller Rings

Pre-string 12 wooden beads onto the brown raffia. Make each ring individually. For each one, cover the ring with 8 stitches, slip a bead, then work 8 more stitches to cover the other half of the ring. Break the thread, leaving 4″ or 5″, and pull it through to secure. Tie the ends, twice, to secure, then use these ends to tie the small circles into the larger ones. Knot on the wrong side 3 or 4 times, touch with clear nail polish and cut away excess threads when dry.

Most tubes of raffia average about 60 to 70 yards. One tube will cover 24 large plastic rings, depending on just how much thread is left on each end for tying. Be sure to purchase enough for your entire project as dye lots can change, just as they do in wool yarns.

COASTERS TO MATCH PLACE MATS

Materials

Brown raffia straw
No. 5 plastic crochet hook
7 plastic rings, ⅝″ in diameter
6 brown wooden beads, 10mm

LARGE RING

16 SLIP STITCHES

Fig. 14

BEADS

2 SLIP STITCHES

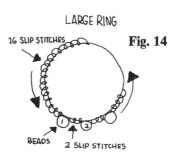

Cover one ring completely with the brown raffia, using 12 stitches but no beads. This will be the center ring around which the other 6 will be added. Pull the raffia through the last stitch to secure, and tie both ends together 3 or 4 times. Trim away excess raffia. Cover 6 rings, adding a brown bead to each, just as you did for the small rings on the place mats—6 stitches, 1 bead, 6 stitches. Break thread, pull through to secure, and knot the two ends of the raffia 3 or 4 times, tightly. Using these ends of raffia, tie the rings around the plain circle, spacing them evenly. With short pieces of raffia (6" or 7" will be long enough), tie the six rings together.

CROCHETED CHRISTMAS TREE ORNAMENTS

Take 5 or 6 to your Holiday hostess. There's always room for a few more baubles on any Christmas Tree!

Materials

16 gold-plated or faceted beads, 8mm size
gold metallic thread
green metallic thread
No. 9 crochet hook
1 large plastic curtain ring, 1½" in diameter

Pre-string the 16 beads to 1 ball of thread. Working both the gold and green threads together, make a chain 5″ long. Still working with double thread, start covering the ring in the usual way for 2 stitches, then slip a bead, work 2 stitches, slip a bead, etc., all the way around. When slip-stitching the beads, use both threads. At the completion of the last bead, join into the 1st stitch with a slip stitch, and make a 5″ chain. Break the thread, and pull it through to secure. Trim off the single threads at the outer ends of each 5″ chain strip, knot and tie the chain strips into a bow at the top of the ring. Attach a small piece of gold thread to the top of the ring to be used for tying the ring to the tree.

CROCHETED KEY RING

Materials

> 10 jeweled beads, 6mm size
> fine gold brocade thread
> No. 3 crochet hook
> 1 plastic or metal curtain ring, ⅞ or 1″ in diameter

Pre-string the 10 beads to the metallic thread, and cover the ring in the usual way. You will work approximately 40 stitches to cover the ring depending on the fineness of the thread used. A heavier thread will use fewer stitches. On the 2nd row around, slip a bead every 4th stitch. When all beads have been used, slip-stitch into the first stitch to close, break the thread, pull it through to secure, and tie it onto a key ring, bringing the thread through the key ring several times before knotting the threads. Secure the knots with nail polish, and trim off the excess threads close to the knots when thoroughly dry.

CHANGE PURSE

To help put an end to the clutter for which a woman's handbag is notorious, make several of these to match your favorite ensembles.

Materials

> 1 ball Knit-Cro-Sheen
> 250 beads (approximately), in contrasting colors, 2 or 3mm size
> No. 4 crochet hook
> 1 zipper, 5″ length

Pre-string 250 beads to the ball of thread and chain 24 stitches.

Round 1 (Add beads on this round). Working on one side of the chain, make a half double crochet in the 2nd chain from the hook. Make 3 more half double crochets in the same stitch. (The 2 chain stitches equal 1 half double crochet, therefore, there will be 5 double crochets in all). Begin with the 1st chain stitch after the 5 double crochets, and make 1 half double crochet, slip a bead, work 2 half double crochets, slip a bead, etc. all the way to the last chain stitch (11 beads in all). Work 5 half double crochets in the end chain. Continue working opposite side into each chain in the same way. End the round by slip-stitching into the 2nd stitch of the 1st half double crochet. This will complete Round 1.

Round 2 (No beads). Chain 2 to equal the 1st half double crochet. Make a half double crochet in each stitch all the way around. To keep your work flat, increase stitches on all no-bead rounds, keeping them evenly spaced.

Round 3 (Add beads on this round). Work a half double crochet into each half double crochet, and slip a bead every other stitch.

Remaining rounds. Work rounds 3 and 4 alternately for 12 rounds in all, ending with a no-bead round. At the end of the last round, break the thread and pull it through to secure. The piece will measure approximately 6¼″ by 4¼″.

Fold the work in half, right sides facing each other. Starting at the bottom of the fold, crochet both sides together for 10 stitches. Repeat for the other side, then sew the zipper across the top opening.

II CROSS-WEAVING PATTERNS

Myriad delightful designs can be created when you work with the needle-weaving technique; some patterns involve 2 needles, others only 1. Either way, it is fascinating to see a design take shape right under your fingertips so quickly. You can change the appearance of an article completely merely by substituting different sizes and shapes of beads and using contrasting colors. The technique, as you will discover, is mathematical and, with this in mind, you will find the patterns a bit easier to understand. The American Indian has been famous for bead weaving for hundreds of years, but his age-old patterns—created in 2mm, 3mm, 4mm and 5mm beads, especially pearls—can be made into handsome contemporary adornments.

Materials and How to Use Them

In addition to the jewelry findings and beads discussed in chapter III, you will need stringing threads in various weights, and fine and medium-fine beading needles. Most 4mm, 5mm, and 6mm beads have fairly large holes, and they will take a darning needle or embroidery needle. Heavier threads, of course, will fit only into heavier needles. Holes in pearls can usually be made larger by inserting the point of an awl or small scissor blade into the hole of the bead and turning it. Crochet thread No. 30 is a good weight for most patterns. Dental floss and pure silk or nylon twist are excellent too. If you duplicate any of the patterns in the tiny seed beads, you will need fine cotton thread. There's no perfect answer to the question of what goes with what except trial and error. Test both needle and thread size. Work a small portion of the design first, to be sure the beads you have chosen will accept the needle and thread. Beeswax (found in Art Needlecraft shops) rubbed over all your threads will virtually eliminate snarls and tangles. Simply pull the entire length of thread across the wax cake. Use white glue (Elmer's) or clear nail polish for securing knots in threads. Make the first knot, add the adhesive to the knot with a toothpick or fine brush, and knot twice more, tightly, to squeeze the adhesive between the strands of thread. When the adhesive is completely dry, trim off the excess threads close to the beads. End threads can be hidden and secured by first applying glue, then feeding the needle and thread back through an inch or so of the design. Trim off the excess threads close to the top of the last bead when the glue is dry.

Working Platform

You will make your work so much easier if you create a simple working platform. Cover a 1″ thick sheet of styrofoam that measures approximately 12″ by 24″, with a smooth piece of material. I use a piece of sheeting. Using straight pins with large heads (corsage pins), pin the fabric over the top of the styrofoam, tightly so that the front surface is free of wrinkles. Also use the corsage pins for fastening your work to the platform. The lightweight "table" can rest on your lap as you work, and you can anchor your needles in the styrofoam so that they will be handy when you need them.

Helpful Hints

When passing a needle back through a bead that is already threaded, stretch the thread with the bead over your index finger. This will cause the thread that is already on the bead to be pulled down to the bottom of the bead hole. If you then pass the needle through the top of the bead hole, you will not run the risk of catching the point of the needle in the thread that is resting on the bottom of the bead hole. Should your needle catch the thread, unthread the needle, remove the thread, re-thread the needle and start over.

You can tint your own pearls in fabric dye if you are unable to buy those that have been commercially colored. Make dye extra strong (2 tablespoons to 1 cup hot, not boiling, water). Let pearls stand, immersed, for 10 minutes. After that, they will absorb no more color. Be sure to rinse them thoroughly in cool water after tinting. Expect colors to be much softer than the dye package shows.

I have tried to set up the patterns so that some of the simpler ones would be at the beginning, and those with similar methods have been grouped together.

48

DAINTY PEARL CHOKER

Materials

1 strand pearls, 2mm size
1 small pearl button
2 beading needles
3 yards No. 30 crochet thread

Put a needle onto both ends of the thread, and sew the small button in the middle of the thread, securing the knots with adhesive. Attach the button to the working platform with an anchor pin.

Center Pattern

String 36 beads onto one needle, and bring the other needle down through the 36 beads, giving them a double thread. * String 6 beads onto the left needle and string 5 beads onto the right needle. Cross the 5-bead needle up through the bottom bead of the 6-needle thread, and pull both threads taut. Repeat from * until you have 14 circles of beads in all. At the completion of the 14th circle, feed 3 beads onto each needle.

Outer Edge

Working up both outer edges of the center pattern, bring the right needle up through the middle bead on the right side of the bottom circle and pull the thread taut. Bring the left needle up through the middle bead of the left side of the bottom circle and add 3 beads to each needle. Continue working up both sides of the center pattern, adding 3 beads between each circle until all but the last circle has been trimmed. Leave the top one untrimmed. Working *down* both sides, feed 3 beads onto the left needle and bring it down through the center bead of the left outside row. Feed 3 beads onto the right needle, and bring it down through the center bead of the right outside row. Repeat for the full length of the pattern. String 49 beads onto the right needle. Make a circle of beads at the end of the 49 beads by bypassing the end 12 beads, bringing the needle down through the remaining 36 beads. Remove both needles and tie both threads together several times, securing the knots with clear nail polish. Cut away both threads close to the beads when the polish is completely dry.

PEARL BRACELET

The bracelet is 7½" long and will fit an average wrist. Increase or decrease 2 or 4 beads, if necessary. To make a matching necklace, merely increase the pattern to the desired length.

Materials

76 pearls, 6mm
36 inches of fine sewing thread
2 fine beading needles
2 gold or silver jump rings
1 spring ring

Cut a yard of thread and tie a jump ring in the center of the thread. Insert a corsage pin into the center of the ring and stick the pin into the working platform. Add a needle to each end of the threads and slip 1 bead onto 1 needle. Pass the other needle down through the top of the bead, giving this 1st bead double thread. Slide the bead close to the jump ring. String 45 beads onto the left needle and 2 beads on the right needle. Push up 3 beads from the left needle. Pass the right needle up through the bottom bead and pull both threads taut, thus forming a circle of 6 beads. The needle and thread with the pre-strung beads should now be on the right. String 2 more beads on the empty needle and thread, push up 3 beads from the pre-strung thread and pass the 2-bead needle up through the bottom bead. Pull both threads taut to form another circle of 6 beads close to the preceding one. The empty needle and thread should now be on the right and the pre-strung beads on the left. Continue in this manner, working from left to right, until the 42 beads have been used and you have made 14 circles of beads. As you cross the working needle from side to side, insert it into the styrofoam platform so that it will be easy for you to find when you need it again. To finish off the 15th circle, insert the 2 bead needle down through the top of the last bead of the opposite thread, giving the last bead double thread. Remove the needles and tie the threads to the small loop on the spring ring, securing the knots with clear nail polish or white glue. Trim off the excess threads close to the knots when they are completely dry.

SCARF NECKLACE

With a minimum of effort and materials, achieve the maximum of fashion with the scarf necklace. It will accommodate a long narrow scarf or a square one.

Materials

 200 beads, 4mm
 10 beads, 6mm or 8mm
 No. 30 crochet thread
 2 beading needles

Fig. 15 ANCHOR PIN

Cut a piece of crochet thread 50″ long and attach a needle to each end. String 10 small beads and slide them down to the center of the thread. Transfer 1 large bead onto 1 needle and bring the other needle up through and to the opposite side. Anchor both needles in the working platform, and pull both threads taut, to form a circle of beads. *Fig. 15.* * Transfer 10 small beads and one large bead to the left needle, and 10 small beads to the right one. Bring the right needle up through the large bead that is on the left needle, pull both threads taut, and repeat from * 8 more times. String 5 beads onto each needle. Bring the right needle up through the 5 beads on the left, and the left needle up through the 5 beads on the right. Apply a small amount of white glue or clear nail polish to both threads, and work the needles back through 1 complete unit on each side to secure. Cut away excess threads when dry. Weave your scarf in and out between the circles.

LACY PEARL CHOKER

This necklace is made in 2 sections, and the 2nd section is joined to the 1st as it is being worked. Make a bracelet to match by working only 6½ or 7″ of the pattern.

Materials

> 202 pearls, 5mm
> 70 oat pearls
> 4 small gold jump rings
> 2 large gold jump rings
> 1 hook
> 4″ chained pearls
> 2 beading needles
> No. 30 crochet thread

Cut 2 pieces of thread 2 yards long. In the center of each, tie a small jump ring. Pin 1 thread to the working platform by putting an anchor pin into the jump ring, then pushing the anchor pin into the platform. Put a needle onto each end of the thread. String 1 round bead to both threads. To the left needle, string 1 round and 1 oat. To the other, string 3 round and bring the needle down through the oat

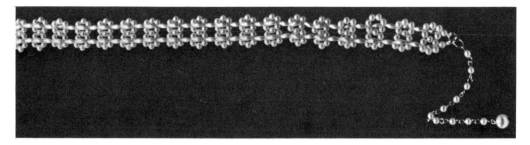

bead that is on the other thread, and pull both threads taut. Repeat with 3 round and 1 oat on the left needle, 3 round on the right needle, bringing the right needle down through the oat bead on the left needle, then pull both threads taut. Continue until the pattern has been worked for 17 circles. For the 18th circle, string 3 round on one needle, 4 round on the other, and bring the 3-bead needle down through the bottom bead of the 4-bead needle. The 18 patterns should measure about 12½ to 13", long enough for an average neck size. Measure your neck to be sure, and keep in mind that the clasp and jump ring closing will add ½" to ¾" to the length, too.

Attach a jump ring to the 18th circle, tying 3 or 4 times, and securing with clear nail polish. When dry, cut off only 1 thread, as you will need only 1 to finish this section of the pattern.

Bring the needle up through the round bead that is next to the jump ring. String 1 oat bead, and bring the needle up through the oat bead that is between the 1st and 2nd circle. String an oat bead and bring the needle up through the next oat bead of the pattern. Continue in this manner to the opposite end. Bring Needle and thread through the jump ring, twice; put nail polish or glue on 1" of thread and bring needle down through the top round bead, then through the next 2 or 3 oat beads. Remove the needle and trim off excess thread when dry.

Pin the 2nd 2-yard piece of thread to the working platform, after knotting a small jump ring to the middle of the thread. Pin the 2nd thread next to the 1st section, leaving about ¼" of space between the 2 anchor pins. Put a needle on both ends of the thread, string 1 round bead to 1 needle and bring the other needle down through the round bead.

* To the right needle, string 3 round and 1 oat. To the left needle, string 1 round, and bring the needle down through the middle round

1   2   3   4   5   6

bead of the right side of the 1st section. String 1 round bead and bring the needle down through the oat bead that is on the right needle. Repeat from * for the entire length and finish the last circle with a round bead on the double thread instead of the oat bead. Knot the thread to a small jump ring, secure with adhesive, cut off threads when dry, and with the remaining needle and thread, add oat beads up the center of each circle, attaching to the top jump ring, just as you did for the first section. You may choose any one of several ways of closing the choker. Ease open the jump rings at both ends, and add one double bar to each. To one double bar, add a jump ring and spring ring; to the other, add a jump ring. If you have chained pearls, use a 3½″ length and attach a jump ring to one end of the chained pearls, using the same jump ring to attach to the 2 jump rings at one end of the choker. Add 1 large pearl to the other end of the chain. Join the 2 rings at the opposite end with another jump ring, and attach a hook to the ring before closing it.

This same pattern can be easily enlarged to belt size by adding 2 or 3 extra rows to either the left or right side of the design, and continuing the pattern to the desired length.

HEADBAND IN SEED BEADS

Our young people have adopted the Indian headband with great gusto. Here's one that is lightweight and comfortable to wear. It is shown in a young-looking red, white and blue color combination, but green and brown earth tones would be equally appropriate. Shorten the pattern to make a fashionable choker too.

Materials

1½ strands blue beads, 10° or 11°
1 strand of red beads, 10° or 11°
1½ strands of white beads, 10° or 11°
1 small button
2 very fine beading needles
fine sewing thread

1   2   3   4   5

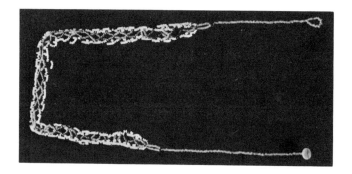

Sew the small button into the middle of 3½ yards of thread. Knot the threads at the base of the button several times, and secure the knots with clear nail polish. Attach to working platform. String 4″ of blue beads to 1 needle, then bring the 2nd needle through in the same direction, thus giving these 4″ of beads a double thread. String 10 blue beads onto the left needle and 9 blue beads onto the right needle. Bring the right needle down through the last bead on the left needle. Repeat 1 more time in blue. Repeat the pattern for 29 circles, alternating red and blue, but make the last 2 in blue to correspond with the starting end. Onto 1 needle string enough blue beads to adjust to the head size you need, about 4″, and, skipping the 20 end beads, bring the needle down through the remaining ones. This will form a loop of beads large enough to hold the button on the other end.

Outer Rows

Bring the right needle up through the beads on the right side of the first blue circle, and the left needle up through the beads on the left side of the same circle. String 5 white beads on the right needle, and insert the needle up through the 5th (middle) bead of the next blue circle. Repeat with 5 more white beads on the left needle on the left side of the same circle. String 5 more white beads on the right needle, and insert the needle up though the 5th (middle) bead of the next circle which will be the first red circle. Repeat with the left needle on the left side of the red circle. Continue all the way to the opposite end, going up through the last 5 beads on each side of the next to last blue circle.

At this point, threads should be tied off and glued. If a narrower headband is desired, leave it as it is. To make a wider one, as shown, another row of white beads has been added to each side. Using another yard of thread, tie the middle of it between the first 2 blue circles at one end, and attach a needle to each end of the thread. Working either up from the bottom or down from the top, string 5 white beads to one needle, bring it through the center bead of the outside row of the 2nd blue circle. String 5 white beads on the other needle and repeat on the other side. Continue to the end of the band, each time adding 5 white beads. Knot the threads, add adhesive to secure, and trim off excess threads when dry.

For the choker, work the pattern for 6½", leaving 12" or 14" of thread at each end. Feed on enough beads at each end to make a proper fit for the neck, and attach a jump ring at one end and a spring ring at the other, securing the knots with adhesive.

PEARL BIB

The bib is shown in 3mm pearls, but it's lovely in gold-plated beads too. For a very delicate effect, follow the same pattern using the small 10° or 11° beads in a color or clear crystal. The length will need to be adjusted to neck size, however, because of the great difference in bead sizes.

Materials

> 6 strings pearls, 3mm size
> 1 medium fine beading needle
> fine crochet thread, heavy duty sewing thread or dental floss
> 1 clasp

Because of the length of the bib, it is impractical to work the entire necklace with one long piece of thread. It is much easier to manipulate by using several pieces 3 or 3½ yards long.

Cut 3 yards of thread, tie one half of the clasp onto one end, and secure the clasp with 2 or 3 knots and glue or clear nail polish. Attach to platform and put a needle to the opposite end, transfer 60 beads to the thread and push them to the clasp.

Row 1: Counting from the needle end of the thread, bring the needle up through the 28th and 29th beads, and pull the thread through.

Fig. 16 (A). Feed on 10 beads, push them down the thread, skip the next 10 beads of the original 60 beads, and bring the needle up through the next 2 beads. *Fig. 16 (B)*. Feed on 8 beads, push them down the thread, skip the next 8 beads of the original 60 beads, and bring the needle up through the next 2 beads. Feed on 6 beads, skip the next 6 beads of the original 60 beads, and bring the needle up through the remaining beads of the original 60. Pull the thread after each addition so that the beads are close together. You will have created 4 triangles of beads. This is the foundation of your pattern and completes the first *up* row.

Row 2: Working down, feed on 6 beads, skip the first 2 beads, and bring the needle down through the 3rd and 4th beads of the first triangle. Feed on 6 beads, skip the first 2 beads of the 2nd triangle, and bring the needle down through 3rd and 4th beads of the 2nd triangle. Feed on 8 beads, skip the first 3 beads of the 3rd triangle, and bring needle down through the 4th and 5th beads of the 3rd triangle. Feed on 10 beads, skip the first 5 beads of the last triangle, and bring the needle down through the 6th and 7th beads.

Row 3: Working up, feed on 20 beads, skip the first 4 beads of the nearest triangle, and bring the needle up through the 5th and 6th beads. Feed on 8 beads, skip the first 3 beads of the next triangle, bring the needle up through the 4th and 5th beads. Feed on 6 beads, skip the first 2 beads of the next triangle, and bring the needle up

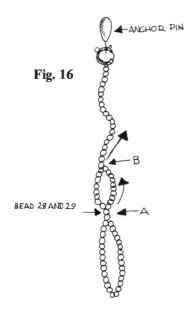

Fig. 16

ANCHOR PIN

B

BEAD 28 AND 29

A

through beads 3 and 4. Feed on 6 beads, skip the 1st 2 beads of the next triangle, and bring needle up through the 3rd and 4th beads.

Now your pattern is set. Every other row is worked up, and every other row is worked down. The even numbers are down, and the odds are up. The next row will be the 4th. Follow the directions for Row 2. For the 5th row, follow the directions for row 3, etc., until you have reached the desired length. The one shown has 45 bottom loops (triangles), and will fit an average neck size. When more thread is needed, apply white glue or clear nail polish to the thread, work through the last few beads of the pattern at the point where you need to add thread, and trim off the old thread close to the bead when the thread is completely dry. Start a new length of thread at the point in the pattern where the previous thread ended, knot the end of the new thread, cover the knot and the first 2″ of thread with nail polish, and continue with the pattern. Trim off knot when thread is completely dry.

When the desired length has been completed, tie on the other half of the clasp, add adhesive to the thread, knot twice again, and weave the needle and thread back through the last inch or two of the pattern to reinforce. Trim off thread very close to the beads when dry.

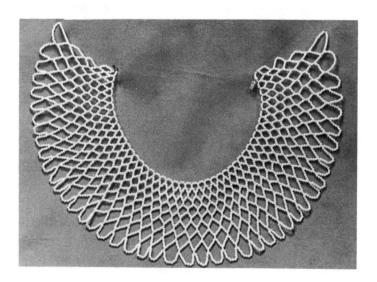

PEARL AND OAT BEAD NECKLACE

Materials

480 round pearls, 5mm
128 oat pearls
fine crochet thread
2 beading needles
1 clasp

Cut 2 pieces of thread 3 yards long and add a needle to each. Attach one half of the clasp to each of the other ends, using both threads, and secure the knots with adhesive. Pin the clasp end at the top of the working platform so you will be working vertically, and string 4 round pearls to the left needle. String 2 round beads to the right needle, and cross the right needle from right to left, through the 4th bead of the left needle, and pull both threads taut so as to form a 6 bead circle of beads. *Fig. 17.* Now the needle that started on the right side is on the left side of your work, and the left needle becomes the right one. Repeat by stringing 4 round beads on the left needle, and 2 on the right needle. Cross the right needle from right to left, through the 4th bead of the left needle, and pull both threads taut to form a 2nd circle of 6 beads. *Fig. 18.* Continue until 30 more circles have been made, 32 in all. Use one needle and thread to attach the 2nd half of the clasp, securing the knots with clear nail polish, and cutting off the excess thread when dry.

Turning the working platform so that its length is horizontal, attach the other end of the necklace to the platform so that it forms a horizontal line.

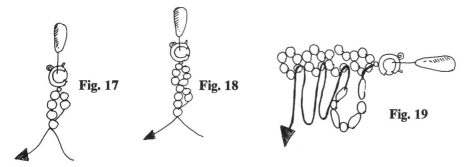

Fig. 17   Fig. 18   Fig. 19

Working from right to left, bring the remaining needle and thread through the first 2 beads to the left of the 2nd half of the clasp. String 1 oat, 1 round, 1 oat, 1 round, 1 oat, 1 round and 1 oat. Bring needle through the 1st bead of the next circle. String 1 oat, 1 round, 1 oat, 1 round, 1 oat, 1 round and 1 oat, and bring the needle through the 1st bead of the next circle. *Fig. 19.* Repeat until all 32 circles have been worked. Cover an inch or so of the thread with clear nail polish, and bring the needle through the beads of the end circle to secure. Cut off excess thread when dry.

PEARL AND OAT BEAD BIB

Materials

384 round pearls, 4mm
384 oat pearls
1 clasp
1 beading needle
No. 30 crochet thread

Cut 3½ yards of thread, and to one end tie on one half of a clasp, securing the knots with adhesive. Attach a beading needle to the opposite end of the thread and mount the clasp end to the working platform with an anchor pin. String 1 round, 1 oat, 1 round, 1 oat, 1 round, 1 oat, 1 round, 1 oat and 2 round beads.

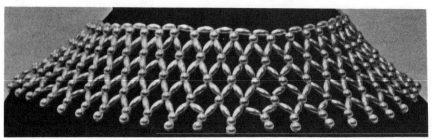

Row 1: Skip the bottom round bead, and bring the needle up through the 2nd bead from the bottom, pulling the thread all the way through. String 1 oat, 1 round and 1 oat. Skip 1 oat, 1 round and 1 oat, and bring the needle up through the next round, *Fig. 20,* pulling the thread all the way through, thus forming a triangle of beads. String 1 oat, 1 round, 1 oat, skip 1 oat, 1 round, 1 oat, and bring the needle up through the top round. Pull the thread all the way through to form another triangle of beads. This completes the first *up* row of the pattern.

Row 2: String 1 oat, 1 round, and 1 oat. Bring the needle down through the first round of the top triangle. *Fig. 21.* String 1 oat, 1 round and bring the needle down through the round of the second triangle. Pull the threads all the way through. String 1 oat and 2 rounds, and bring the needle up through the 2nd round, skipping the bottom round. Now you are ready to repeat Row 1. Each *up* row is an odd number and each *down* row is an even number. Continue working the pattern until there are 49 double rounds at the bottom. Attach the 2nd half of the clasp and secure with adhesive, cutting off excess thread when dry.

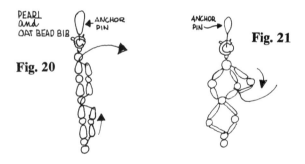

PEARL *and* OAT BEAD BIB ← ANCHOR PIN   ANCHOR PIN →   **Fig. 21**

Fig. 20

ORANGE AND YELLOW NECKLACE

Working with more than 1 color is a bit more complicated, but the effects you can achieve are worth the extra effort. This pattern uses at least 5 yards of thread, so I suggest it be made with 2 pieces 2½″ to 3″ long, working the pattern as far as possible with 1 thread, then securing the 2nd thread to continue on to the end.

Materials

2½ strands of yellow opaque beads 2mm, each strand 60" long
1 strand orange opaque beads 2mm, 60" long
No. 30 crochet thread
1 fine beading needle
1 clasp

Row 1: Attach a needle to one end of a 3 yard piece of thread, and to the other end, tie on one half of a clasp, securing the knots with adhesive. Attach the clasp end of the thread to the working platform with an anchor pin. String 2 yellow, 2 orange, 6 yellow, 2 orange, 6 yellow, 2 orange and 6 yellow beads and push them to the anchor pin.

Row 2: Working from the bottom to the top, and along the right side of the beads, bring the needle up through the 2 yellow beads that are directly under the 2 orange ones, and pull the thread through. *Fig. 22.* String 2 orange and 4 yellow beads, bring the needle up through the 2 yellow beads that are under the next 2 orange beads, and pull the thread through. *Fig. 22 (B).* String 2 orange beads and bring the needle up through the 2 top yellow beads. *Fig. 22 (A),* pulling the thread through each time.

Row 3: For the 3rd row, working down the right side of the 2nd row, string 5 yellow, 2 orange and 4 yellow beads. Bring the needle down

Fig. 22

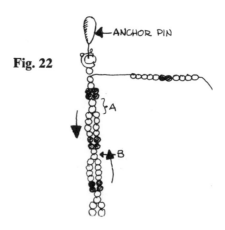

through the 2 yellow beads that are directly above the second 2 orange beads. String 2 orange and 4 yellow beads, and bring the needle down through the 2 yellow beads that are above the third 2 orange beads. String 2 orange and 6 yellow beads and bring the needle up through the 2 yellow beads that are under the last 2 orange beads, just as you did for Row 2. Now your pattern is set. For row 4, repeat row 2, and complete it by bringing the needle up through the first 2 yellow beads above the top 2 orange beads. You will find that by starting each *down* row with 5 beads, each pattern will be separated by 3 beads across the top. If you prefer a tighter fit to the necklace, start each *down* row with 4 beads instead of the 5. Continue repeating the pattern, weaving up and down, until the desired length has been completed. The necklace shown has 43 points at the bottom, and will fit an average neck size. Attach the 2nd half of the clasp to the finished end, and secure it with adhesive, cutting off the excess threads when dry.

GOLD TEARDROP NECKLACE

This regal design calls for beads in 3 different sizes, and although the method is very much like several others already explained, the effect is utterly different. Pearl rounds, oats and teardrops can, of course be substituted instead of the all-gold beads.

Materials

67 gold-plated beads, 6mm
198 gold-plated oat beads
33 gold teardrops
No. 30 crochet thread
1 beading needle
1 clasp

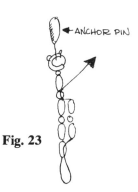

Fig. 23

Tie one half of the clasp to one end of a 3-yard piece of thread, and attach a needle to the other end. Secure the clasp to the working platform with an anchor pin. String 1 oat, 1 round, 1 oat, 1 round, 2 oats and 1 teardrop.

Row 1: Worked up. Bring the needle up through the oat bead that is directly above the teardrop, and pull the thread all the way through. String 1 oat, 1 round, 1 oat, and bring the needle up through the top round bead. *Fig. 23.*

Row 2: Worked down. String 1 oat, 1 round and 1 oat and bring the needle down through the next round of the 1st row. String 2 oats and a teardrop, and bring the needle up through the oat bead that is directly above the teardrop. This is the start of row 3, and is worked just like row 1. Repeat the pattern, alternating the pattern of row 1 for all *up* rows, and the pattern for row 2 for all of the *down* rows, until you have added 33 teardrops. Work the last *up* row, and tie on, with adhesive, the 2nd half of the clasp, trimming off excess threads when dry.

GOLD TEARDROP EARRINGS

Materials

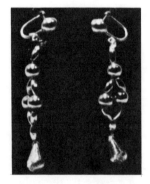

> 8 gold-plated beads, 6mm
> 12 gold-plated oat beads
> 2 gold teardrops
> 2 earring backs
> No. 30 crochet thread
> 1 beading needle

String 1 oat, 1 round, 1 oat, 1 round, 2 oats and a teardrop. Bring the needle up through the oat bead that is directly above the tear-

VII. Poppies, 13" high, 17" wide, p. 162.

VIII. Place mats and coasters, p. 42; arrangement with cone flowers, p. 170; cat-o-nine tails, p. 169; and painted dahlias, p. 165. Overall size, 18" high, 20" wide.

IX. Christmas candles, p. 149; Christmas tree balls, p. 148.

drop. String 1 oat, 1 round and 1 oat, and bring the needle up through the top round and top oat. Tie onto earring backs, securing the knots with clear nail polish. If your earring backs have a small cup on the top, glue a round gold bead to each.

WOVEN BRACELET IN BLUE AND WHITE

Once the procedure is mastered, any combination of colors may be worked into this design. White and blue opaque beads were used here, and a spring ring closing may be substituted for the beaded loop and button one. Makes a great gift item.

Materials

> 3 strands white opaque beads, 11°
> 1½ strands blue opaque beads, 11°
> 1 single strand clasp or 1 beaded 8mm bead
> strong, fine sewing thread
> 2 fine beading needles

Row 1: Cut 45″ of thread and fold it in half. Wrap at least 12″ of the folded end around the head of an anchor pin and attach it to the working platform. Thread a needle to each open end, and string 12 white beads onto 1 needle. Bring the other needle and thread down through the 12 beads, thus giving the 12 beads double thread. Cover the threads with a light coating of clear nail polish as you work, applying it to both threads an inch or so at a time. This will stiffen the threads just enough to give the bracelet a hollow, tubular effect when it is completed. String 6 white beads onto the left needle, and 5 white beads onto the right needle, pushing the beads close to the base of the original 12 beads. Bring the right needle up through the bottom bead of the left thread, crossing the right needle to the left side. Pull both threads to form a small circle of beads. *Fig. 24.* Again, string 6 white to the left needle, 5 to the right needle, bring the right needle up through the bottom bead of the left needle, and pull the thread through. Pull both threads taut to form a 2nd circle. *Fig. 25.* Repeat for 1 more circle with white beads. Transferring to the blue beads, make 4 more circles in blue, then transfer back to the white beads for 20 circles. Work 4 more circles in blue, and 3 more in white. At the completion of the 3rd white circle, string 12 white beads to 1 needle and bring the other needle through, so that the 12 beads will be on double thread. Remove both needles and knot the threads, twice, close to the last beads, and secure the knots with adhesive.

Row 2: Start another 45″ of thread, just as you did for row 1, and anchor it to the working platform next to the 1st row of the pattern. String 12 beads on double thread, pushing them up close to the anchor pin. String 2 white beads to the left needle, and bring the left needle down through the middle bead (3rd) of the right side of the 1st circle of row 1. String 3 more beads to the left needle. String 5 beads to the right needle, and bring the right needle up through and to the left of the bottom bead on the left thread. *Fig. 26.* Pull both threads taut to form a circle of beads. Make 2 more circles in the same way, still using the white beads. Continue in the same manner, making 4 circles with blue beads, 20 circles with white beads, 4 with blue, and 3 with white, attaching them to the 1st row as you work. String 12 white beads to one needle, and bring the 2nd needle through from top to bottom, so as to give the 12 beads a double thread. Remove both needles, and knot the 2 end threads, twice, close to the base of the 12 beads.

WOVEN BRACELET IN BLUE AND WHITE

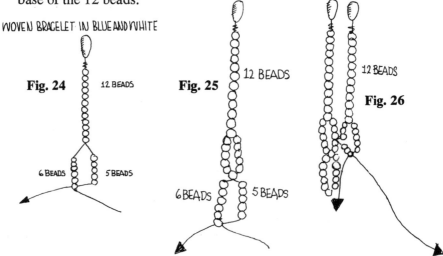

Fig. 24   12 BEADS

Fig. 25   12 BEADS

12 BEADS

Fig. 26

6 BEADS   5 BEADS

6 BEADS   5 BEADS

Rows 3 and 4: Repeat the directions of row 2 for rows 3 and 4. After finishing row 4, string the end 12 beads on needle only. Remove the needle from the thread and make a sewing knot at the end

66

of the thread to keep the 12 beads on the thread. Leave the needle on the 2nd thread, as this will be used to join the 2 outside rows.

Remove the bracelet from the working platform, cut open the end loops of the threads at the top, and knot them together by dividing them in half, and tying them twice, close to the top of the four 12-bead strands. Be sure to secure the knots with clear nail polish. Separate 2 of the threads, choosing the 2 longest ones, and attach a needle to both. Onto 1, string 30 white beads. Bring the 2nd needle through, thus giving the 30 beads double thread. Remove the needles, and tie the 2 threads at the top of the four 12-bead strands. This will form a loop of 30 beads, thus making one half of the bracelet closing. Cut off excess threads when dry.

At the opposite end of the bracelet, tie together all but the thread with the needle, securing the knots with nail polish. Trim off all but 1 of these threads when dry and put a needle on this one. This needle will be used to make a beaded ball after the bracelet has been sewn together.

Insert an anchor pin into the 30-bead loop, and attach the bracelet to the working platform. The one needle and thread that remains should be on the lower right, at the bottom of the 4th row of the bracelet. String 3 white beads, fold the bracelet in half, lengthwise, and bring needle up through the middle bead of the last circle of the first row to the left. Repeat in the same manner, working from left to right, adding 3 beads as you work, for the full length of the bracelet. Change from blue beads to white ones as you come to them in the pattern. When the last circle has been joined, bring the needle up through the nearest 12-bead strand and string on one 8mm bead. String 8 white beads, and bring the needle up through the large bead again. String 8 more beads, needle up through again. Repeat 3 more times, until you have 5 rows of 8 beads each on the large bead. Remove the needle. Bring the second needle up through the large bead, repeat for 5 more rows of 8 beads each, and remove the needle. Tie both threads together at the top of the bead, securing with nail polish. Cut away excess threads when completely dry.

ROPE BRACELET

There are several other articles that use this same method, but, because the bracelet is worked all in pearl and does not have a contrasting color, it will be easier. When working with more than one color, the beads must be pre-strung, but for this design, the original strings may be used.

Materials

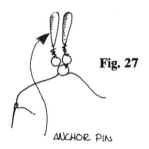

Fig. 27

216 pearls, 5mm
2 medium-size gold filigree caps
2 gold head pins
2 gold jump rings
1 gold spring ring
No. 30 crochet thread or pure silk twist
2 beading needles

ANCHOR PIN

If the pearls are not on thread, cut 2 pieces of thread 30″ long. Put a needle on one end and a securing knot on the other end of each thread. Attach an anchor pin to each, and wrap about 5″ of knotted end of the thread around the base of the head of the pin. Push the pins into the top portion of the working platform about ¼″ apart. String 54 pearls onto the left needle.

If the pearls are already strung, attach one end of the strand of beads to an anchor pin, allowing 5″ of thread at the pin end. Use a 30″ piece of crochet thread for the other anchor pin, and attach a needle to the opposite end of the crochet thread.

Row 1: Working from the pre-strung thread, push up 2 beads. String 1 bead onto the right thread. Bring the right needle up through the bottom bead of the left strand, cross the right needle to the left side, anchor it into the working platform, and pull both threads taut. *Fig. 27.* The beaded thread will now be on the right side and the empty thread to the left. Push up 2 more beads, string 1 bead on the

68

empty thread, bring needle up through the bottom bead, cross the needle to the right side, anchor it to the working platform, and pull both threads taut. *Fig. 28.* Repeat until all 54 beads have been used, and remove the needle. Tie the bottom threads together twice and secure them with clear nail polish. Note: The extra beads that are fed onto the needle one at a time, can be removed from the bottom of the pre-strung strand as you need them, or can be spilled into a saucer.

Row 2: Repeat row 1, setting the 2 anchor pins ¼″ apart and to the right of the first 2 pins. *Fig. 29.* When row 2 is finished, remove the needle and tie the bottom threads together twice, securing with nail polish.

First joining row: Cut a 30″ piece of thread and add a needle to each end. * Push the right needle down through bead, *Fig. 30 (A)* and the left needle down through, *Fig. 30 (B)* and adjust so that both needles have the same amount of thread. String a bead onto the left needle, and cross the right needle up through the bead and to the left. Pull both threads taut. Bring right needle down through bead, *Fig. 30 (C)* and the left needle down through bead, *Fig. 30 (D).* String a bead onto the left needle, and bring the right needle up through the bead and to the left. Repeat from * for the full length of rows 1 and 2. Remove the two needles, and tie the threads together twice to secure.

Second joining row: Cut another 30″ piece of thread and attach a needle to each end. Bring the outer rows of the bracelet together by folding it in half, lengthwise. Starting at the top, join the outer edges together the same as for the first joining row. Tie the 2 bottom threads together twice, to secure. Remove the anchor pins. There will be 4 threads at one end, and 8 at the other. At the 4-thread end, divide the threads in half, 2 and 2, and knot them once, securing the knot with nail polish. At the 8-thread end, divide the threads in half, 4 and 4, and knot them once, securing the knot with nail polish.

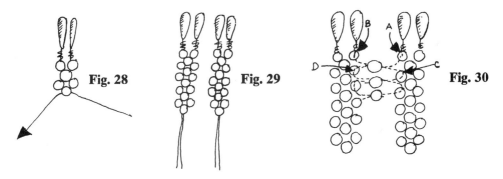

Fig. 28   Fig. 29   Fig. 30

Attach one head pin to each end, knotting the threads twice and securing with polish. Add a filigree cap to each head pin, then add a jump ring to each one. Snip off all but ½" of the open end of the head pins, and using a jewelers' pliers, ring the end of the pin into a circle, slipping the jump ring into the circle just before closing it tightly. To the opposite end, add another filigree cap to the head pin, then a jump ring. Snip off all but ½" of the open end of the head pin, and ring it closed with pliers. Open the jump ring just wide enough to slip on a spring ring, then press it closed again.

PEARL AND GREEN ROPE CHOKER

The method for working this choker is the same as the one used for the pearl rope bracelet, however, this one shows you how and where to add a contrasting color in the pattern.

Materials

    270 pearl beads, 4mm
    90 green transparent or opaque beads, 4mm
    No. 30 crochet thread
    2 beading needles
    2 small gold jump rings
    2 small gold filigree caps
    3 head pins
    4" chained pearls
    1 gold hook
    1 large pearl, 8mm

Attach 2 anchor pins to the working platform with threads and needles to both, using 30" of thread for each needle, the same as for the rope bracelet, earlier in this chapter, *Fig. 27*. You may use the original thread of the pre-strung pearls for the left pin if you wish,

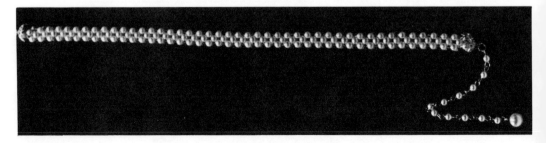

and no needle will be needed, but it is advisable to remove one thread, as they usually come strung on two. Have 90 beads on the left thread, and follow the instructions for Row 1 of the rope bracelet, working to the end of the 90 beads. Follow the instructions for Row 2 of the rope bracelet, using another 90 beads on the left thread of the 2nd row. When working the 2 joining rows, substitute 1 green bead instead of a pearl for the cross-through bead. You will have 4 threads at one end, and 8 at the other. At the 4-thread end, divide the threads in half, 2 and 2, knot them once, securing the knot with nail polish. Divide the 8 strands in half, 4 and 4, and knot them, securing the knot with nail polish. Attach a head pin to each end, tying the threads twice more, securing the knots with polish. Cut away excess threads when completely dry. To one end, add a filigree cap to the head pin, and 1 small jump ring. Cut away all but ½″ of the head pin, and ring it around the jump ring. Open the jump ring just wide enough to attach it to a gold hook, then close the ring tightly. Add a filigree cap and small jump ring to the opposite end. Snip off all but ½″ of the head pin, and ring it around the jump ring. Open the end link of the chained pearl, and hook it into the jump ring, then close. To the opposite end of the 4″ length of chained pearls, attach a large pearl. To prepare the large pearl, slide it onto a head pin, cut away all but ½″ of the open end of the head pin, insert the head pin into the last link of the chained pearls and ring the end of the pin into a tight circle with jewelers' pliers.

MOROCCAN BRACELET IN GOLD

Materials

> 11 jeweled beads, 6mm
> 62 gold-plated beads, 4mm
> 1 large jump ring
> 1 large spring ring
> 2 beading needles
> 1 yard No. 30 crochet thread

Cut a 1-yard piece of thread, tie a spring ring to the center of the thread, securing it with 3 knots and clear nail polish. Place a needle on each end of the thread, and attach the clasp end to the working platform with an anchor pin. String 1 small bead to one needle and bring the other needle down through the same bead, giving the bead

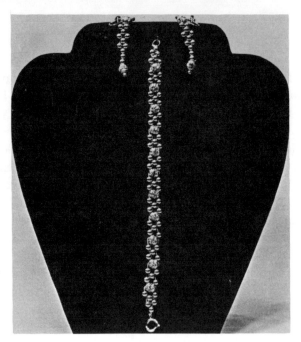

a double thread. To the left needle, string 3 small and 1 jeweled beads until you have used 11 jeweled beads, each one separated by 3 small beads, then finish by adding 4 more small beads.

* String 1 small bead on the empty thread (right), push up the 2 top beads from the left thread, bring the right needle up through the 2nd bead, and cross the needle to the left. Pull both threads taut. String 1 small bead onto the empty thread; it is now on the left side of your work, push up the next 2 beads from the other strand (1 small and 1 jeweled), and bring the other needle up through the 2nd bead (jeweled) crossing the needle to the right. Repeat from * until there are 2 small beads left. String 1 small bead on the empty thread, and bring the needle down through the last bead, giving the bottom bead a double thread. Tie on a large jump ring, securing the knots with adhesive, and cut away excess thread when dry.

MOROCCAN EARRINGS IN GOLD

Materials

    2 earring backs with small front cups
    4 jeweled beads, 6 mm
    22 gold-plated beads, 4mm
    4 gold-plated beads, 2mm
    2 beading needles
    25" of No. 30 crochet thread

Attach a needle onto each end of the thread, and string one 2mm gold bead to the middle of the thread. Onto 1 needle, string 1 jeweled bead, and bring the 2nd needle down through the jeweled bead, giving the jeweled bead double thread. Onto the left needle string 8 small 4mm gold beads, and anchor the needle into the working platform. String one 4mm bead to the right needle, push up 2 beads from the left thread, bring the right needle up through the 2nd gold bead, crossing the needle to the left. Pull both threads taut. Push up 2 more beads, string a 4mm bead onto the empty thread, and bring the needle up through and to the right. Pull the threads taut. String one 4mm bead on the empty thread, and bring the needle down through the last three 4mm beads, giving them double thread. Remove one needle and tie both threads together twice, tightly, securing with adhesive. Onto the remaining needle, string 1 jeweled bead and 1 small 2mm bead. Skip the small bead, and bring needle up through the jeweled one. Remove needle and tie both threads together, twice, securing with polish. Cut away excess threads when dry. Set a drop of Duco cement into the small cup of the earring back and glue the top jeweled bead to the cup. Repeat for the 2nd earring.

MOROCCAN NECKLACE IN GOLD

Materials

2 gold-plated beads, 8mm
381 gold-plated beads, 4mm
45 jeweled beads, 6mm
1 clasp
2 small filigree gold caps
2 gold head pins
2 small gold jump rings
2 beading needles
No. 30 crochet thread

Fig. 31

Neck Band

Cut 2 pieces of thread 1 yard long, add a needle to each one, and join the opposite ends of the thread with a sewing knot. Wrap at least 12″ of the knotted end of the thread around an anchor pin, and attach the pin to the working platform. Onto 1 needle, string 1 large 8mm gold bead, and 20 small ones. Bring the 2nd needle down through, so that all 21 beads are on a double thread. String 1 small gold on the right needle and 2 small gold on the left one. Bring the right needle up through the bottom bead on the left thread, crossing the right needle to the left side. Insert both needles into the working platform, and pull both threads taut, bringing these 3 beads up close to the base of the strand of 21. String 1 small on the right needle, 1 small and 1 jeweled bead on the left one. Bring the right needle up through the jeweled one; pull both threads taut. String 1 small on the right, 2 on the left, bring the right needle up through the bottom bead on the left, and pull the threads taut. String 1 on the right, 2 on the left, bring right needle up through the bottom left bead, and pull the threads taut. String 1 gold on the right, 1 gold bead and 1 jeweled bead on the left, bring right needle up through the jeweled bead, and pull the threads taut. String 1 gold on the right, 2 on the left, and bring the right needle up through the bottom left bead, pulling the threads taut. String 1 gold on the right and 1 gold and 1 jeweled and 3 gold on the left needle. Bring the right needle *down* through the second gold, the 1 jeweled bead and the 3 remaining gold ones. These last 5 beads are now on double thread. To 1 needle, string 1 jeweled, 1 gold, 1 jeweled, etc., until there are 6 jeweled beads, each one separated by 1 small gold. Bring the 2nd needle through these beads to give them a double thread. To 1 needle, string 3 small gold, 1 jeweled, and 1 small gold, then bring the other needle through to give these beads a double thread. Onto the right needle, string 1 gold, on the left one string 2 gold, and bring the right needle through the 2nd gold, pulling the threads taut, as usual. Repeat with 3 more gold beads. String 1 gold on the right, 1 gold and 1 jeweled on the left, and bring the right needle through the jeweled bead. String 1 gold on the right, 2 gold on the left, and bring the right needle through the 2nd gold bead. Repeat with 3 more gold beads. String 1 gold on the right, 1 gold and 1 jeweled on the left, and bring the right needle up through the jeweled bead. Repeat 1 more time with 3 small gold beads.

Onto each needle, string 1 gold bead. Onto 1 needle, string 20 gold beads and the other 8mm bead. Bring the other needle down through so that these 21 beads are on double thread. Remove both needles, wrap the 2 threads around another anchor pin, and insert the pin into the working platform, turning the platform so that its length is horizontal, and the necklace is taut across the center.

Pendant Design

Row 1: Cut a 30″ piece of thread and add a needle to each end. Bring one needle through the first jeweled bead of the center pattern (neck band), pushing it through from right to left. *Fig. 31 (A).* Pull the thread far enough so that there is an even amount of thread on both needles. * Put 1 small bead on the right needle and 2 on the left. Bring the right needle up through the bottom bead of the left thread, and pull both threads taut. Repeat from * 3 more times, 4 in all.

String 1 small bead on each needle and 1 jeweled bead on the left. Bring the right needle up through the jeweled bead, and pull the threads taut. Repeat the pattern 3 more times with the small beads, then string 1 small bead on each needle, and bring both threads down through a jeweled one.

Remove one needle, knot the 2 threads at the base of the jeweled bead, securing the knots with clear nail polish.

To the remaining needle, string 10 small beads, 1 jeweled bead, and 1 small bead. Skip the bottom small bead, and bring the needle up

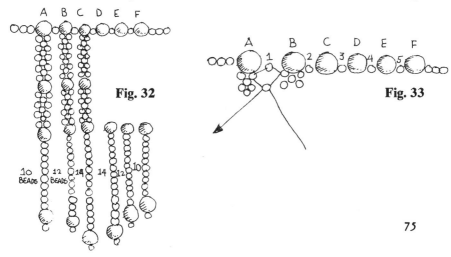

Fig. 32

Fig. 33

75

through the jeweled bead and the 10 small ones. Pull thread tightly so as to keep the beads close together. Remove the needle and tie together, twice, the 2 threads that are below the top jeweled bead that is above the 10 small beads, securing the knots with nail polish. Cut away all but 1″ of threads. They can be trimmed closer when the threads are completely dry.

Repeat this procedure on each of the jeweled beads, but on the second one, *Fig. 32 (B)* string 12 small beads, 1 jeweled, and 1 small. At *Fig. 32 (C)* and *(D)*, string 14 small, 1 jeweled, and 1 small. At *Fig. 32 (E)*, string 12 small, 1 jeweled, and 1 small, and at *Fig. 32 (F)*, string 10 small, 1 jeweled, and 1 small.

To the first small bead, *Fig. 33 (1)*, attach thread and 2 needles the same as for the jeweled bead. You will now be joining the pendant pattern. Bring the right needle down through the first small bead under, and to the left of, the 2nd jeweled bead of the top neck band. Bring the left needle down through the first small bead that is under, and to the right of, the 1st jeweled bead. String 1 small bead to the left needle, bring the right needle up and through, and pull the threads taut. Bring the right needle down through the next small bead on the right, and the left needle down through the next small bead on the left. Add a small bead to the left needle, cross the right needle up through it. Repeat 2 more times, 4 in all, joining rows A and B as you work. Repeat the pattern 1 more time, using a jeweled bead for the cross-through bead. Repeat the pattern 3 more times using small beads for the cross-through bead. Bring the needles down through the last pair of small beads, and bring both needles down through a jeweled bead. You now have joined row A to row B. Remove 1 needle and knot the threads once, securing the threads with nail polish, and to the remaining needle, string 11 small, 1 jeweled, and 1 small. Skip the bottom bead, and bring the needle up through the 1 jeweled bead and the 11 small ones. Remove the needle, and tie both threads twice, securing the knots with nail polish. Repeat this procedure, joining row B to row C, row C to row D, row D to row E, and row E to row F, but to row 2, string 13 small, 1 jeweled, and 1 small; to row 3, string 15 small, 1 jeweled, and 1 small; row 4, string 13 small, 1 jeweled and 1 small; and to row 5, add 11 small, 1 jeweled and 1 small.

To each end of the necklace, tie on 1 gold head pin, securing the knots with nail polish. Push the knots close to the head of the pin.

Trim away excess threads when dry. Onto each head pin, place a small-sized gold filigree cap. To one end, put a large jump ring. Cut away all but ⅓″ of the open end of the pin and ring the pin closed, around the jump ring. To the other end of the necklace attach a spring ring, and ring the open end of the head pin around it, closing the ring tightly.

MOROCCAN EVENING PURSE

This same pattern can be worked for a less formal look in wooden beads or faceted plastic ones. Increase the size to a full handbag if you wish. Learn the technique from the Moroccan necklace or bracelet, and adapt it to suit your needs.

Materials

1750 (approximately) gold-plated beads, 4mm
50 gold jeweled beads, 6mm
1 zipper, 6″ long
2 beading needles
No. 20 crochet thread or fine nylon twist

The materials listed are the amounts needed to make a purse that measures 7″ wide and 2¾″ down, fringe not included in measurements. Use a ready-made zipper bag or make your own gold brocade, velvet or satin: This size comfortably holds eyeglasses, lipstick, keys, drivers' license, handkerchief, small change and folding money, too. The beads are worked in 1 long section with fringe on the first 7″ only. This will give you fringe across the front of the purse, leaving the back plain. However, if you want fringe across the back, too, work it for the full length.

Basic top row. Cut a 30″ piece of thread, put a needle on one end and attach an anchor pin to the opposite end, using 6″ or 7″ of thread around the base of the pin. With the working platform set vertically, fasten the anchor pin to the top of the platform. String 1 small bead, 1 jeweled bead, 1 small bead, etc., until you have used 35 small beads and 34 jeweled ones, alternately. Remove the needle, wrap the thread around a 2nd anchor pin, turn the working platform to a horizontal position, and attach the 2nd anchor pin to the platform so that the string of beads is stretched tightly across the platform in a straight, horizontal line.

First down row. **Cut a 24″ piece of thread and attach a needle to both ends. Bring 1 needle from right to left, through the 1st jeweled bead on the left of the basic top row. Pull the thread through so that there is an even amount of thread on each needle. * To the left needle, pre-string 22 small gold beads. String 1 small gold bead to the right needle, push up 2 beads from the left thread, and bring the right needle, from left to right, through the 2nd bead on the left. Pull both threads taut so that the 3 beads of the pattern are close to the bottom of the 1st jeweled bead. This is the same method used for working the rope bracelet. *Fig. 27.* Repeat from * until the 22 pre-strung beads have been used. To the left needle, string 1 jeweled bead, and bring the right needle down through the jeweled bead, giving the bead a double thread.

Fringe

To the left thread, string 5 small beads, 1 jeweled bead, and 1 small bead. Skip the bottom small bead, and bring the needle up through the bottom jeweled bead and the 5 remaining small beads. Cover both threads with nail polish, and tie the threads together, tightly, close to the base of the jeweled bead at the top of the fringe. Remove needles, and cut off excess threads close to the beads when they are completely dry.

Repeat from **, treating each jeweled bead in the same way, until half of them have been worked. This will complete the front of the purse. If you wish fringe across the bottom of the back of the purse also, repeat it all the way across.

First joining row. Join the 1st and 2nd rows the same as for the rope bracelet, using 20″ of thread and 2 needles. It will take 11 small beads. Follow *Fig. 30.* When the joining row has been completed, cover 1″ of both threads with nail polish, and back weave each needle up through the rows of beads on either side of the joining

row for an inch or so, to secure. Remove needles and cut off both threads close to the beads when completely dry. Continue to join each down row with a joining row, all the way across.

Attaching to Lining

Remove the purse from the working platform, and with needle and matching thread, sew the top of the purse around the top of the zippered lining. Remove the anchor pins from both ends, attach a needle to each thread, and, with a joining row, close the two open ends of the beading. Secure by back weaving up through the beads after having put nail polish on the threads. Tack on the bottom of the purse to the bottom of the lining, all the way around, just above the fringe.

RED AND WHITE BELT

This belt measures approximately 60″ in length, tasseled ends not included. It can be worn as a necklace, as is, or shortened. The pattern is the same as the one used for the rope bracelet and the rope necklace, with one exception. It has been left open after the first 2 rows have been joined, and therefore it will lie flat.

Materials

1058 pearl beads, 4mm
530 red beads, 4mm
crochet thread No. 30
2 beading needles

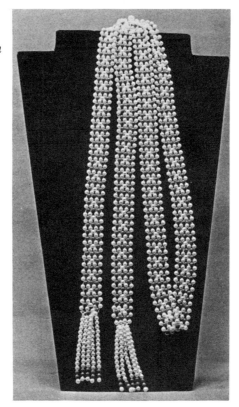

Row 1: Because the belt is so very long, the right side of the unit will be worked in at least 2 sections. Measure 10 or 12 yards of thread, wrap it around a cardboard tubing from paper toweling, and keep it in reserve, to be used when extra thread is needed. Cut another 4 or 5 yards, wrap 10″ of one end around the base of an anchor pin, and attach the pin to the top of the working platform. Put a needle on the opposite end. Add a needle to the ball of thread and pre-string 1 pearl, 1 red, 1 pearl, 1 red bead until you have used 204 pearl beads, each one separated by 1 red bead. Remove the needle and wrap the open end of the thread around the base of another anchor pin, using at least 10″ of thread, and attach this 2nd anchor pin to the working platform, setting it to the left of the first pin. * Put 1 pearl onto the empty thread that is on the right, push up 1 pearl and 1 red bead from the left thread, close to its anchor pin, and bring the right needle up through the red bead. Draw the thread all the way through, then pull both threads taut. Repeat from * for the entire length. When you have used nearly all of the thread on the right needle, apply clear nail polish to the thread, and weave the needle up through an inch or so of the left side of the pattern. Cut away excess thread when completely dry. Re-thread the needle with another 4 or 5 yards of thread from the reserve thread, knot the open end, apply clear nail polish to the first few inches, bring the needle down through the last inch or two of the pattern on the right side, and continue working the pattern to the end. Remove the needle; allow 10 or 12″ of bare thread, and tie the 2 bottom threads together twice, securing the knots with nail polish.

Row 2: Repeat the instructions of Row 1 for Row 2, setting the 2 new anchor pins ¼″ to the right of the 1st two pins of Row 1, and tie the bottom threads together in the same way.

Row 3: Cut 5 yards of thread, fold it in half, and wrap the folded end around an anchor pin, using 10 or 12″ of double thread. Set the anchor pin in between the anchor pins of Rows 1 and 2. Place a needle on each end of the thread, and join Rows 1 and 2 the same as for the rope bracelet, by bringing the right needle down through the top left bead of Row 2, and the left needle down through the top right bead of Row 1. Alternate 1 red bead, 1 pearl bead, 1 red bead, etc. for the cross-through beads, working all the way to the end of the belt. If you wish, you may use all pearl or all red for the cross-through beads. Any one of the 3 methods makes an attractive pattern. The belt shown uses alternates. If you need more thread, back-weave again, securing the threads with nail polish, and start with a new thread at the point where you finished the first one. However, no anchor pin is necessary. Merely bring the right needle down through the first available bead on the right, and the left needle down through the first available bead on the left side, then continue joining the 2 rows as before, all the way to the end. Remove the needles, tie both threads twice, securing each knot with nail polish. You will have 6 threads at both ends. The belt is, of course, much longer than your working platform. In order to take full advantage of the platform, work 12 or 15 inches of the belt, lift it, and secure it with an anchor pin or two, work another 12 or 15 inches, lift it, and secure it again.

Tassel

Using the 6 threads at both ends of the belt, build the 1st tassel on the end you have just finished. Working 1 thread at a time, add a needle, string 12 pearls, 2 red, and 1 pearl. Apply nail polish to the thread, skip the bottom pearl, and bring the thread up through the 2 red beads and the 12 pearls. Remove the needle. Repeat for the other 5 threads, and cut off excess threads when completely dry. Remove the anchor pins from the opposite end of the belt, and make another tassel. Cut open the thread that was folded in half, and this will give you 6 threads at this end, too.

BRAIDED GOLD AND PEARL BELT

This belt is adaptable. It can be made into a necklace. For the necklace, shorten the design to whatever length you desire. Two such stunning belts are in *Color Plate No. II* and *No. III*. One is done in blue and white seed beads, and the other in 3mm pearl and gold-plated beads. The materials for the gold and pearl belt are listed.

Materials

4 strands pearls, 3mm size (approximately 560 beads to a strand), 60" to a strand
1120 gold-plated beads, 3mm
1 beading needle and No. 30 crochet thread
4 small gold filigree caps
4 gold head pins
8 gold jump rings
6 gold-plated or pearl teardrops
12" chained pearls

Join 2 strands of pearls by tying their strings together at both ends. Tie them so that the pearls are not tight between the knots. Repeat wih 2 more strands. The gold-plated beads are not usually strung, so it will be necessary to string them. On 2 pieces of thread, each measuring 75″, string approximately 560 gold beads to each thread and tie them together at both ends.

Allowing 4″ of thread at one end, tie twice, all 6 of the threads, securing the knots with glue or clear nail polish. When dry insert an anchor pin (corsage pin) just below the knot. Stretch all 6 strands so that they are parallel to one another. Have 2 strands of pearls on either side of the 2 gold ones. Braiding on a carpeted floor may sound ridiculous, but it works like a charm. Insert the anchor pin into the carpeting at one end of a room, push all beads up to the anchor pin, and braid for the entire length, treating each of the 2 strands as 1. When the braiding is finished, tie all 6 of the open end strands together, 3 times tightly, slipping a gold head pin into the 2nd knot. Apply adhesive to the 2nd and 3rd knots and trim off the excess threads when dry. Attach a gold head pin to the opposite end in the same way, secure with adhesive and cut off the threads when dry.

Tassel

Make 2 tassels: Separate the 12″ of chained pearls into 6 pieces, each 2″ long, by opening the joining links with a jewelers' pliers. Put three 2″ pieces onto a head pin and bend the head of the pin into a circle to secure the chained pearls. Insert the open end of the head pin up into the center of a filigree cap. Cut off all but ⅓″ of the head pin and ring the open end into a circle to secure. Open the bottom links of the chained pearls with a pliers, and attach either a gold-plated teardrop or a pearl one. If the gold teardrops have no shank to hook into, add a small head pin, close it, and then add the chained pearls. Add a tassel to each end of the belt with a small jump ring.

III BOUTIQUE JEWELRY

Combining jewelry findings with beads can be most gratifying because you can easily change designs to your needs of the moment merely by opening links to remove old sections, or adding new ones. Here is where you can let your imagination run wild.

Choosing the proper materials and becoming familiar with the mechanical elements involved is a most important part of any project. Much of the equipment needed here is also used in other chapters of the book. For example, a sharp-nosed jewelers' pliers is absolutely necessary for assembly of all the jewelry items, and you'll also find the pliers very helpful in twisting the wires on the beaded flowers. In working with the jewelry findings, 2 small pliers are much easier to work with when opening and closing rings, but a sturdy tweezers can take the place of the extra pliers, and work very well.

Take special note of the necklace design that includes the instructions for knotting between each bead. This should be of great value to you the next time your favorite strand of pearls breaks, especially if it happens on a weekend when the repair shop is closed.

There are, of course, hundreds of items of jewelry findings that are used by professional costume jewelry designers and manufacturers, but the ones listed here are the most workable in the designs you will be following. Chains, jump rings and filigree caps, for example, come in a wide range of sizes, but I recommend that you keep your needs as simple as possible. Suggested are small, medium and large gold filigree caps, jump rings in small and medium, spring rings in small and medium and two styles of earring backs. I use 1¼" head pins because they seem to work to the best advantage. You'll not always need the full length, but the short pieces you cut away can very often be used for shaping small jump rings or joining smaller beads. There are clasps for single, 2-, 3- and 4-strand necklaces. I chose to use the plainer ones that do not detract from the design itself, but this is really a matter of personal taste, and the more elaborate ones are available if you prefer them. The following chart shows actual sizes. *Fig. 34.*

Most of the beads that are used in the patterns you will find in any craft and hobby shop, and in the Art Needlework departments of large stores, and all of them come in a wide range of sizes. Beads are graded in millimeters (mm for short), and the smaller the number, the smaller the bead. Those most adaptable to our purposes are 2, 2½, 3, 4, 5, 6, and 8mm, with an occasional 12 or 18mm for a special effect. Pearl beads can be purchased either loose, in small packets, or on 60" strings. The number of beads to each string will vary with the size of the bead. For example, there will be more 2mm beads than 4mm beads to a single strand.

The Beads

The oval pearls (oat beads) come either strung or loose, the same as the round pearls. Gold-plated beads, moonstones, teardrops, jeweled and plastic-faceted beads usually come unstrung, and are bought in bulk, in small packages. The amount in each package will vary according to the policy of the company that retails them. The chart below shows the actual sizes. *Fig. 35.* Teardrops usually come with a shank that has a small hook on the small end of the bead. The shank in nothing more than a head pin ringed at one end, so should you need a teardrop with a gold shank, and the ones you have are in silver, snip off the hook end, push out the head pin and put a gold head pin up through the bottom of the tear drop, then ring the end with pliers. Rondels are like very small wedding bands ¼" in diameter. The band is ⅛" wide and is encrusted with jewels. They are available in all jewel tones, emerald, ruby, sapphire, etc., and usually come in packets of 8 or 12.

Chained Pearls

These are usually 3mm pearls joined with gold links, and you can purchase them by the foot or yard, or you can make your own with pearls and head pins by inserting a pin into a pearl, snipping off the head of the pin, forming a ring at each end of the pin, then joining to another pearl and head pin. There are usually 3 pearls to an inch.

84

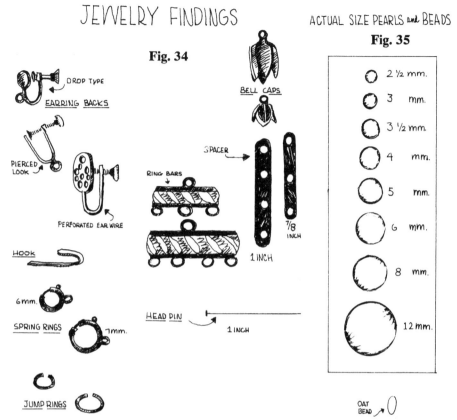

JEWELRY FINDINGS

Fig. 34

DROP TYPE

EARRING BACKS

PIERCED LOOK

PERFORATED EAR WIRE

HOOK

6mm.

SPRING RINGS   7mm.

JUMP RINGS

BELL CAPS

SPACER

RING BARS

7/8 INCH

1 INCH

HEAD PIN

1 INCH

ACTUAL SIZE PEARLS and BEADS

Fig. 35

2 ½ mm.

3   mm.

3 ½ mm.

4   mm.

5   mm.

6   mm.

8   mm.

12 mm.

OAT BEAD

Jump Rings

These are used for joining. To open a jump ring, have the cut section of the ring facing up. Grasp both sides of the opening with either 2 pliers or 1 plier and a tweezer, then gently turn one plier away from you, and the other plier toward you so as to widen the opening just enough to slip on a chain link, clasp or ring. Jump rings are usually added to a spring ring closing on a bracelet or necklace, as this will make opening the spring ring easier. When the end beads of a bracelet, for example, are too close to the clasp, there is too little space, and it can be difficult to get your fingers close enough to operate the clasp with ease. Jewelry is more graceful, and will hang better, too, with proper spacing.

Spring Rings

These are excellent for closings on small bracelets and necklaces. A small or medium sized jump ring attached to the opposite end of the necklace is the other half of the clasp into which the spring ring will hook.

Head Pins

Inserted into the beads, these can be used with the heads left on to keep the beads from slipping off, as in the tassel of *Pattern No. 12;* or with the head snipped off. When the head is snipped off, both protruding ends of the pins bent into a ring with the jeweler's pliers will permit you to add links, clasps, etc. wherever needed. This method is called "ringing a head pin."

Link Chains

Cut into various lengths, these chains determine the dimensions of many of the designs. They are available in many weights, but a medium fine one was used on all of these designs.

Spacers

These are used to keep rows of beads in a straight line so they won't sag. They are used mostly on chokers like *Pattern No. 11.*

The designs in this chapter have only numbers to guide you. The method for combining the parts is the same on all.

NECKLACE PATTERN No. 1

Materials

  18" medium fine gold chain
  12 pearls, 8mm
  8 gold head pins, 1¼" ea.
  24" (approximately) of chained pearls

Cut 12 pieces of gold chain, each piece measuring 1½". Prepare 6 of the 8mm pearls with 1 head pin for each. To do this, center each pearl on a head pin, and snip off both ends of the pin, leaving no more than ⅓" on both ends. *Fig. 36.* With jeweler's pliers, bend each'end into a semi-closed ring, close to the bead. *Fig. 37.* To each end, attach a 1½" piece of chain and close the ring on each side of the pearl. This will make 6 sections.

Working with the chained pearls, count 5 pearls and open the ring at the 5th pearl, count 5 pearls and open the ring at the 5th pearl, etc., until you have 12 sections of 5 pearls each.

86

Prepare the 6 remaining 8mm pearls with head pins, and to each end attach a 5 bead section of the chained pearls.

Combine all 6 sections, alternately, and close the ends. The necklace will be approximately 28" long.

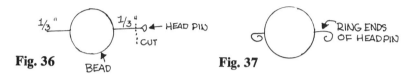

Fig. 36   BEAD   Fig. 37

BRACELET PATTERN No. 2
Companion Piece to Necklace No. 1

Materials

10 pearls, 8mm size
9" gold chain
3 small gold jump rings
1 gold spring ring
10 gold 1¼" head pins

Bracelet

Prepare 6 pearls with head pins *(see Pattern No. 1, Fig. 37)*. Cut 5 pieces of gold chain 1" long. Join the pearls and the pieces of 1" chain alternately, starting and ending with a pearl. Attach a small gold jump ring to both ends and a gold spring ring to one end for the clasp.

Tassel

Cut 4 pieces of gold chain 1″ long. On one end of each piece of chain, attach a pearl and head pin. To prepare the 4 remaining pearls, slide each onto a head pin, pushing the beads to the head of the pin. Snip off all but ⅓″ from each pin, add a 1″ piece of chain to each, and close the ⅓″ of the head pin into a closed ring to secure the last link of chain.

Open a jump ring just wide enough to receive the end links of the gold chains to which the pearls have been added. Before closing the jump ring, attach it to the jump ring that adjoins the spring ring clasp, then close it tightly.

Make a pair of earrings to match, using just the tassels attached to earrings backs.

NECKLACE PATTERN No. 3

Materials

> 21½″ gold chain
> 22 pearls, 8mm
> 22 gold head pins
> 3 large gold jump rings
> 2 small gold jump rings
> 1 large spring ring in gold

Prepare all 22 pearls with head pins (See Pattern No. 1, Fig. 37.) closing the rings only partially. Cut 10 pieces of gold chain, each 2″ long. Starting with 2″ of chain, add a pearl, 2″ of chain, 1 pearl, 2″ of chain, 1 pearl, 1 large jump ring, 2″ of chain, 1 pearl, 2″ of chain, 1 pearl, 2″ of chain, 1 pearl, 2″ of chain, 1 large jump ring, 1 pearl, 2″ of chain, 1 pearl, 2″ of chain, 1 pearl, and end with 2″ of chain. To one end of the combined units, add 1 small jump ring and a spring ring. To the other end, add 1 small jump ring and a large jump ring. The large jump rings in the centers of this basic chain will be used to attach the upper and lower swags.

Upper Swag

Cut 7 pieces of gold chain ½″ long. Starting with ½″ of chain, add a pearl, ½″ of chain, add a pearl, etc., until 6 pearls have been

added, and end with ½" of chain. Open the large jump rings that are in the middle of the basic necklace, and add one end of the upper swag to each ring. Leave the jump rings partially open, and make the lower swag.

Lower Swag

Cut 8 pieces of chain 1" long. Starting with 1" of chain, add a pearl, 1" of chain, add a pearl, etc., until 7 pearls have been added, each pearl separated by 1" of chain, and finish with 1" of chain. Attach each end to the same jump ring that holds the upper swag, and close the jump rings tightly.

JEWELED NECKLACE PATTERN No. 4

Materials

> 21" of gold chain
> 28 yellow moonstones, 4 mm
> 14 orange moonstones, 4 mm
> 28 white opaque beads, 4mm
> 70 gold head pins

Prepare all of the beads by centering each one on a head pin, snipping off the head of the pin, and ringing each end. *Fig. 37.* Join them together in the following sequence; * 1 white, 2 yellow, 1 white, 2 orange, 1 white, 2 yellow, and 1 white. Repeat from * until you have 7 sections.

Cut 7 pieces of chain 3″ long and starting with 3″ of chain, attach a bead section, then 3″ of chain, a bead section, etc., until all have been joined together. Join the two open ends.

NECKLACE PATTERN No. 5

Materials

> *29 gold jeweled beads, 6mm*
> *30″ of gold chain*
> *29 gold head pins*

Prepare all 29 gold jeweled beads with head pins; reduce the length of the head pins to ¾″ by snipping off the excess at the head end.

Center the beads on the ¾″ of pin, and ring both ends of the pin. Cut 29 pieces of gold chain 1¼″ long. Starting with a jeweled bead, attach a 1¼″ piece of chain, then a bead, then chain, etc., until all have been joined including the ends. Your necklace will be approximately 25″ long.

JEWELED NECKLACE PATTERN No. 6

Materials

    30 emerald green jeweled rondels
    15 jeweled beads, 8mm
    15 gold head pins, 1¼″ in length
    30 small jump rings
    30″ gold chain

Snip off the heads of all 15 head pins. * Ring 1 end of 1 pin with the pliers and put 1 rondel on the open end, then 1 large jeweled bead, and 1 rondel. Ring the other end of the pin to secure. Repeat from * until you have 15 units.

Cut 15 pieces of gold chain 2″ long, and to each end of each piece of chain add 1 small jump ring.

Starting with a jeweled bead unit, attach a jump ring and chain unit. Attach another bead unit to the other end of the chain, alternating bead units and chain units until all have been joined, then close the two ends. The necklace will be 22″ long when completed.

GOLD AND RUBY NECKLACE PATTERN No. 7

Materials

>9 gold and ruby jeweled beads, 6mm
>9 gold and ruby jeweled beads, 8mm
>20 gold head pins
>31½ yards of gold chain

Prepare each jeweled bead on a head pin, snipping off the heads of the pins and ringing the ends of the pins to secure the beads to the pins. *Fig. 37.* Cut 18 pieces of chain 1¾″ long. Starting with a large bead, add a piece of chain, 1 small bead, a piece of chain, 1 large bead and a piece of chain until all have been joined, and end with a chain. Join the open ends.

NECKLACE PATTERN No. 8

Materials

>24 silver jeweled beads, 6mm
>8 silver jeweled beads, 8mm
>20″ of silver chain
>32 silver head pins
>16 small silver jump rings

Cut 16 pieces of chain 1¼″ long. Starting with 1 small bead, mount it on a head pin, insert the open end of the head pin into the end link of 1 piece of chain, and ring the pin with pliers to close it into a circle. Push the bead down close to the circle, snip off ½″ of the opposite end of the head pin, slide a small jump ring onto the pin, ring the open end of the pin around the jump ring to close. Put

another small bead onto a head pin, insert the open end of the pin into this same jump ring, and ring the pin around the jump ring to close. Push the bead close to the jump ring, snip off ½″ of the opposite end of the head pin, slide on another jump ring and ring the head pin around the jump ring to close. Put another bead on a head pin, attach it to the 2nd jump ring, snip off the other end, slip on a piece of chain and ring the pin around the 1st link of the chain. Make 7 more units the same way. Join all 8 units with the 8mm jeweled beads by putting each large bead on a head pin, snipping off the head of each pin, and ringing each open end of the pins through the end links of the chains.

DANGLE NECKLACE PATTERN No. 9

Materials

6 pearls, 5mm
1 large pearl, 8mm
3 pearl teardrops
10 gold head pins
2 small jump rings
1 large jump ring
1 large spring ring
21″ gold chain

Prepare the 6 small pearls on head pins, snipping off all but ¾″ at the head end, and ring both ends of the pins. *Fig. 37.* Cut 6 pieces of chain 2″ long, and one piece 4″ long. Starting with 2″ of chain, add a small bead to one end, then add 2″ of chain, 1 bead, 2″ of chain, 1 bead, 4″ of chain, 1 bead, 2″ of chain, 1 bead, 2″ of chain, 1 bead, and end with 2″ of chain. To one end, add a small jump ring and a large jump ring. To the opposite end, add 1 large spring ring.

In the center of the 4″ piece of chain, attach a small jump ring through the middle link of the chain, and close the ring.

Dangle

Prepare the large bead with a head pin, but snip off the head of the pin. Ring one end through the small jump ring in the center of the 4″ piece of chain. Ring the other end of the pin partially closed. To this partially closed ring you will add the rest of the dangle.

Cut 2 pieces of gold chain 1½″ long, and 1 piece 1¾″ long. Attach a teardrop to one end of each piece of chain, and hook the other ends of the chains into the partially closed ring at the bottom of the pearl; then close the ring.

DANGLE EARRINGS PATTERN No. 9

Materials

2 large pearls, 8mm
4 pearl teardrops
4 gold head pins
4½" gold chain
2 small cupped gold earring backs

Slide 1 head pin into an 8mm pearl and leave the head on the pin. Onto the other end of the pin, hook 1 piece of 1" chain, 1 piece of 1¼" chain and another piece of 1" chain in that order. Ring the pin closed. Attach a pearl teardrop to the open ends of each chain. Glue the 8mm pearl to the cup of the earring back. Repeat for the other earring.

SPUTNIK EARRINGS PATTERN No. 10

Materials

2 jeweled sputnik balls
7" gold chain
4 small round jeweled beads, 4mm
2 small jump rings
8 gold head pins
2 small cup earring backs

Cut 6 pieces of gold chain 1" long, and set aside. Prepare 6 small gold jeweled beads with head pins by sliding a bead onto each one. Put a head pin onto the end link of a 1" piece of chain, snip off half of the open end of the pin and ring it around the end link to close. Repeat with the remaining 5 jeweled beads and chain. * Snip off the head of a head pin, add the open ends of 3 beaded chains and ring the head pin to secure the 3 chains. Onto the opposite end of the head pin, put 1 large jeweled sputnik bead and 3 links of gold chain. Ring the end of the pin to secure the chain. Join the 3 links of gold chain to a gold earring back with a small jump ring, and glue a small jeweled bead to the cup of the earring back. Repeat from the * for the other earring.

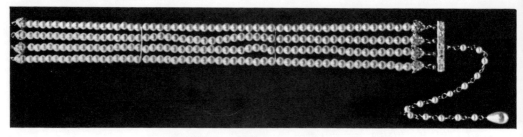

PEARL CHOKER PATTERN No. 11

Materials

216 pearls or moonstones, 5mm
5″ chained pearls
2 spacer bars, 4-hole
8 small filigree gold caps
2 bar clips, 4-ring
10 small jump rings
1 teardrop
1 gold hook
large eye beading needle
thread, crochet No. 30, pure silk or nylon twist

* Cut a 30″ piece of thread and knot one end to a head pin, knotting at the base of the head, tightly, 3 times, securing the knots with white glue or clear nail polish. Put a needle on the other end of the thread, and string 18 pearls, the outside hole of a spacer bar, 18 pearls, the outside hole of a spacer bar and 18 pearls. Remove the needle and knot around the head of another head pin, securing the knots with adhesive. Repeat from * 3 more times. Make sure the 2nd strand goes through the hole of the spacer bar that is adjacent to the one already used. The 3rd strand should go through the next hole, and the 4th strand through the outside one. Trim off excess threads when the adhesive is dry.

Working at one end of the choker, add, 1 at a time, a small filigree cap, then a small jump ring to each strand. Ring the open end of each pin around each jump ring, to close. Open the jump ring just wide enough to hook it into the corresponding loops of the 4-ring bar. *Fig. 38.* Close the jump ring tightly. Repeat on the other ends of the strands with 4 more caps and 4 jump rings, attaching them to another 4-ring bar.

To one end, add a jump ring and a hook to the single loop of the 4-ring bar. To the opposite end, attach a 5″ piece of chained pearl with a small jump ring. To the open end of the 5″ of chained pearl, attach a pearl teardrop by opening the end loop of the chained pearl and hooking it into the loop at the top of the teardrop.

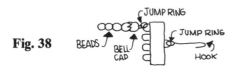

Fig. 38

CHOKER AND ROPE NECKLACE PATTERN No. 12

Materials

90 pearls or moonstones, 5mm
120 pearls or moonstones, 8mm
10 small filigree gold caps
2 medium filigree gold caps
10 gold head pins
2 small gold beads, 3mm or 4mm
2 gold bar clips with 3 holes each
64" fine gold chain
1 embroidery or darning needle
pure silk or heavy nylon twist

Choker

* Cut a 25" piece of thread and tie one end to a head pin, 3 times, securing each knot with white glue or clear nail polish. Thread a needle to the opposite end and string on 30 of the small beads. Remove the needle and tie on another head pin close to the last bead. Be sure to have the beads tight on the thread, and close together. Knot the thread 2 more times, securing the knots with adhesive. Repeat from *, making 2 more strands in the same way. To both ends of each strand, and working one at a time, add a small filigree cap to each head pin. Snip off and discard half of the head pin, then ring the end with pliers to secure the cap. To each ringed head pin, attach a small jump ring, and before closing the ring, attach a 3-loop bar. To the single ring on the opposite side of each bar, add a jump ring. *Fig. 39.*

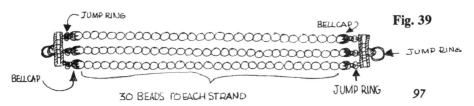

Fig. 39

Rope Ends

Make 2. Cut 65″ of heavy nylon twist or pure silk twist. The thread you choose depends on the size of the bead hole. If the hole is a large one you should use the heavy nylon twist. For the smaller hole, silk twist is fine. Because you will be knotting the thread between each bead, you must make sure the thread you use will make a large enough knot to separate the beads. If the knot is too small, the bead will slip past it, disappear inside the hole, and then, of course, there's no object in knotting at all. Real pearls are always knotted between each bead, and knotting gives a more expensive look to any necklace. Knot the beads in any of the patterns, but keep in mind that the knots take space. Therefore you will not need as many beads as the original pattern calls for, to make the same length.

To one end of the 65″ length of thread, tie on a head pin, and knot it 3 times, securing the knots with adhesive. Add a needle to the opposite end and be sure to use the strongest needle the beads will take. You will be using the needle for leverage against the beads as you tighten the knots. Transfer 1 large bead to the thread, and push it to the head pin. Close to the bead, wrap the thread around the first 2 fingers of your left hand, *Fig. 40,* and bring the needle up through the circle of thread. Set the middle of the needle close to the bead, grasp bead and needle with thumb and forefinger of the left

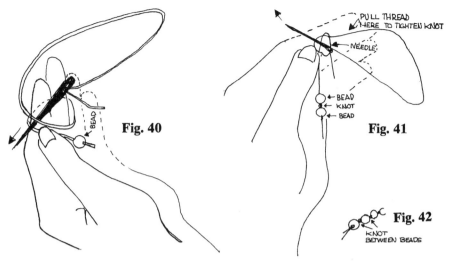

Fig. 40

PULL THREAD
HERE TO TIGHTEN KNOT

NEEDLE

← BEAD
← KNOT
← BEAD

Fig. 41

Fig. 42

KNOT
BETWEEN BEADS

hand, ease the middle finger out of the circle of thread, gently, so you won't disturb the loop of thread. Pull the long thread nearest the bead, easing out the remaining finger as you close the loop of thread. Hold the needle firmly against the bead, *Fig. 41,* and pull the thread tight to completely close the knot. Remove the needle. The knot should be close to the bead. You may feel the needle revolve, slightly, as you close the knot. Continue knotting, one bead at a time, until you have 60 beads, each one separated by a knot. *Fig. 42.* When all 60 beads have been added, tie on another head pin, knotting 3 times, and securing each knot with adhesive. Repeat with 60 more beads for the other rope.

To the head pins on each end of both strands, add 1 small filigree cap. Press the caps over the end beads, firmly, securing them to the end beads with clear nail polish, if you wish. Snip off all but ½" of the open end of the head pin, slip on a small jump ring and ring the pin over the jump ring with the pliers to secure. Hook 1 end of each rope unit to the single ring of the 3-ring bars to which the choker units have been attached.

Tassel (Make 2)

Cut 16 pieces of gold chain 4" long. Put a small 3mm or 4mm bead onto a head pin. Find the middle link on 8 pieces of 4" chain and set the middle links onto the head pin, one at a time. Add a medium size filigree cap, insert the head pin into the small jump ring at the open end of a rope unit, ring the head pin with the pliers and close it tightly. Make another tassel with the other 8 pieces of 4" chain in the same way, adding it to the other rope unit. Should the ends of the tassels have some strands of chain that hang lower than others, snip them off to equal lengths.

This necklace is made so that the choker unit is worn on the front of the neck. The rope units can either be looped at the back of the neck to hang down the back, or be crossed over, brought to the front, and looped.

IV BEAD FLOWERS AND VEGETABLES

GENERAL INFORMATION

Flower arrangements featuring many kinds of flowers with only one of each kind, are not pleasing to the eye because there is no focal point. Instead, choose all of one kind, or make three or four of each different variety for a really striking effect.

This section of the book deals with glass beads only and they are available in the following categories: transparent, opaque, lined, processed, and iridescent. The transparent beads are just that: clear colored glass with a permanent color. Processed beads have a glossy, pearlized finish. Opaque beads, often called chalk, are solid, and no light shines through them; and lined beads are clear crystal beads that have a painted lining to give them their color. Prolonged exposure to strong sunlight may cause them to fade somewhat after a few years, so use lined beads sparingly. Iridescent beads have a "rainbow" effect. All beads are fast color with the exception of the lined ones, and all are washable.

Bead sizes and shapes fall into separate categories. The type you will be using most are perfectly round, and the most universal size is labeled 11°. A 10° bead is larger and will not give your work as smooth an appearance. The 12° bead is very tiny, and very often will not take the 26 and 28 gauge spool wires you will be using. Beads can be obtained already on thread. They are much easier to work with, as it is a simple process to transfer them directly from thread to spool wire. Loose beads are time-consuming to string as each bead must be picked up, one at a time, and transferred to the wire. Threaded beads come in bunches of usually 12 strands to a bunch, each strand measuring about 20-inches long.

All of these small beads are imported, most of them coming from Japan, Czechoslovakia, France and Italy. The French are noted for the soft, muted tones of their beads, while the other countries specialize in brighter, more vibrant colors. All are of equally fine quality.

Colors of beads are ordered by number, but it's much easier for you to tell one from the other if they have names that resemble familiar things. For example, if a bead is referred to as ruby, it resembles the jewel, etc. Dye lots can vary from one shipment to the other, just as yarns and threads do, so buy enough of each color to finish the project you are working on, so there will be a consistent color blend.

Selecting Tools and Other Materials

You will need a heavy duty wire cutter for heavy stem wires, a small wire cutter for the finer spool wires (although a folding nail clipper will do the job fairly well for a start), and a small, long-nosed jewelers' pliers for twisting the wires.

Spool wires come in several weights. You will need 26-gauge for all large flower parts, 28-gauge for medium and small parts, and 32-gauge for lacing and assembling. Stem wires must be strong enough to hold the weight of the flowers. Most will use 16-gauge. Very large flowers will require 12 and 14-gauge and small ones will do well on 18 or 19-gauge.

Floral tape is used for assembling. It comes in a wide range of colors, but those used most are green, light green, twig and brown.

Non-hardening modeling clay is the best substance to use in filling your containers. Styrofoam is not firm enough to keep heavy flowers upright. Cover the clay with sheet moss or a new material called wood moss. It is finely chopped sawdust, tinted several shades of green and it has an oil base that gives it a soft feeling. Press it into the top of the clay and it will cling and remain colorfast, too.

Containers should complement your flowers and not take away their beauty. A bowl or vase that is "too busy" in design will certainly detract from the flowers. Keep them simple but elegant, and when using your fine china pieces or silver, try to find a smaller bowl that will fit into it so that the containers can still be washed or polished. When the time comes to wash the flowers, if they are in a liner, merely turn them upside down in a container of water that is deep enough to immerse the flowers, swish in mild soap, then rinse in lukewarm clear water. In no time they will be dry, and sparkle like new.

METHODS

Study the techniques and try them, one at a time, with practice beads and wire before you actually attempt a flower. Try several pointed leaves before doing a flower whose petals are pointed. Leaves can be hidden in an arrangement, and if some of them are not perfect, they will go unnoticed in a bouquet, but petals will stand out.

If this is your first try at bead flowers you will be all thumbs. This is perfectly normal. All beginners feel a bit frustrated at the start. Your fingers will soon master the tiny beads and stubborn wire and soon you will be able to execute every pattern with great deterity.

Keep your finished flower parts separated from strung beads as they have a nasty habit of entangling themselves in the threads of the beads and in no time you will have more loose ones than strung ones. If you spill beads, the best way to pick them up is to moisten the tip of a finger, press it into the beads and pick them up one at a time.

When beads are strung to the wire, you are ready to start. Once you have a knowledge of the techniques that are involved, you can create on your own, changing the counts and measurements. However, follow the prescribed patterns first before striking out on your own.

The techniques that you will need to execute the designs on the following pages are illustrated with step-by-step drawings. They are: Basic, Basic Loop, Round Petals, Pointed Petals and Leaves, Continuous Single Loops, Continuous Wraparound Loops, Continuous Crossover Loops, Shading of Petals, Lacing, Beaded Stems, Assembly and Use of Floral Tape, Stem Wires, Reducing Wires, Split Basic, Single Split Basic, Double Split Basic, and Reverse Wrap.

Stringing Beads on Wire

Open a spool of wire. If you are working with a wooden spool, put a thumbtack in the top of the spool to anchor the wire, so that it won't spiral off. Cut the open end of the wire at an angle to achieve a good point. The beads will feed onto the wire much easier, too. Gently ease out one end of a strand of beads from the bunch. Insert the open end of the spool wire into the beads, then remove the thread from the beads that are already on the wire.

Don't take too many beads at a time; an inch or so is plenty. After a little practice, you'll find that the stringing will go very quickly, and you will accomplish a great deal without even looking. When you have transferred half a strand of beads, make a knot in the end of the string large enough to prevent the beads from slipping off the open end. Gently pull the opposite end of the string and continue removing beads from this new open end. This method will prevent too much spillage of beads. It is seldom necessary to string more than 3 or 4 strands at a time. More can be added as needed.

Should you run out of beads before finishing a leaf or petal, allow enough bare wire to finish the unit, cut the wire from the spool and continue feeding beads onto the open end of the wire until you have enough to finish the unit, crimping the end of the wire to keep the beads from slipping off the open end.

Unless otherwise specified:

> *Never work with a precut piece of wire.*
> *Always work directly from the spool of wire.*
> *Always complete each petal or leaf before cutting the wire from the spool.*
> *Crimp the open end of the spool wire after the required number of beads have been strung on the spool.*

Basic Technique

This is the one you will be working with the most to make individual petals and leaves. The word "basic" when followed by a number or measurement, denotes how many beads or inches of beads to put on the center wire, around which the remaining rows of beads will be wrapped.

Making the Basic Loop

Transfer a strand of beads to a spool of wire, *Fig. 43,* and crimp the open end of the wire. Move the required number of beads to within 4″ of the crimped end of the wire. Hold your work from underneath so that your hands won't hide it. Place your left thumb and forefinger under the wire and to the right of the basic beads. Place your right thumb and forefinger under the wire and to the left of the remaining beads on the wire. *Fig. 44.*

104

Keep the spool wire to the right. Have at least 5″ of bare wire between your fingers. Bring your forefingers together, as in *Fig. 45,* and transfer the basic beads and wire to your right thumb and forefinger. With your left hand, twist together the loop of bare wire that is under your right thumb and forefinger. Twist 4 or 5 times very tightly at the bottom of the basic beads, thus closing the basic loop of wire at the top. Starting on the left side of the basic beads, bring beaded wire up the left side of the basic beads, wrap bare spool wire once around the bare wire at the top of the basic beads (where the single wire is) *Fig. 46,* then bring beaded wire down the right side of the basic beads, and wrap bare spool wire around the loop wires at the base of the basic beads. Wrap only once. Always cross the bare spool wire across the front, to the back, and around to the front again, and wrap firmly. *Fig. 47.*

Continue wrapping beaded spool wire around the basic beads until you have the number of rows called for in your pattern. Keep the rows of beads and the beads themselves close together, and wrap bare spool wire, top and bottom, once tightly, at the completion of each row of beads. The less wire you have showing, the more solid the effect will be and your units will be firmer, too. As you work, keep the basic row of beads straight, through the middle. Don't let it bend in either direction. Keep the right side of your work facing you as you wrap. (After the first few rows have been made, the right and wrong sides will be obvious to you as much more wire shows on the wrong side). To determine the number of rows, count the rows of beads across the center, making sure to count the basic row in your total. The single wire is always considered the top of your petal or leaf, and the loop the bottom. Always finish a unit at the bottom unless specific instructions say otherwise. When finishing at the bottom, you will have an odd number of rows. Should a pattern call for finishing at the top, you will have an even number of rows.

Round Petals

A beginner always finds the round petals easier to make, so let's practice a few. Make a basic of 5 beads, round top and round bottom, 7 rows. As you wrap the bare spool wire around the top and bottom wires, keep the wire close to the row of beads that precedes it. Each pattern has been figured mathematically to achieve the proper dimensions, therefore don't create roundness by leaving spaces between the rows of beads. Keep each new row of beads close to the one next to it. As you make the first wrap at the top of the basic beads, cross the bare spool wire in front of the top basic wire, so that the spool wire is horizontal and at right angles to the top basic wire. *Fig. 46.* Push wired beads to the top of the basic beads. Turn the petal counterclockwise (to the left) with the left hand so that the loop of wire is at the top. Wrap bare spool wire around the loop of basic wire, at right angles, just as you did at the top, around the single wire. *Fig. 47.* Turn your work counterclockwise again, and repeat, wrapping at the top and at the bottom until the seven rows have been completed.

As each petal and leaf is finished, cut the top basic wire ¼" from the top beads and bend the ¼" of wire down the wrong side of the unit. Tuck it in neatly, making sure it doesn't protrude. Allow 4" of bare spool wire and cut the wire from the spool. For petals, cut open the basic loop of wire on one side of the loop. *Fig. 48 (A).* For a leaf, cut the loop open at the bottom of the loop, as most leaves will attach more firmly if they have a 3-wire stem. *Fig. 48 (B).*

Pointed Petals and Leaves

Some have pointed tops and round bottoms, others have round tops and pointed bottoms. Wherever the point, the method for making the point is the same as for a round one, with one exception. To create a point, go two beads beyond the top of basic beads before wrapping the wire, and change the angle of the spool wire to a 45° angle in relation to the basic wire. Push the beads from the spool into the point, and shape it by squeezing the rows of beads together, then flattening the rows so that they do not overlap one another. See *Fig. 49* and *Fig. 50* for pointed tops and bottoms.

Once the point has been started, it must be kept, or the effect is lost, so repeat the procedure each time you work to the point. For a bottom point, start the point at the end of the 3rd row. For a pointed top, start the point at the end of the second row.

Continuous Single Loops

Many flowers are made with continuous loops, each loop worked close to the preceding ones. To make small centers for flowers, count

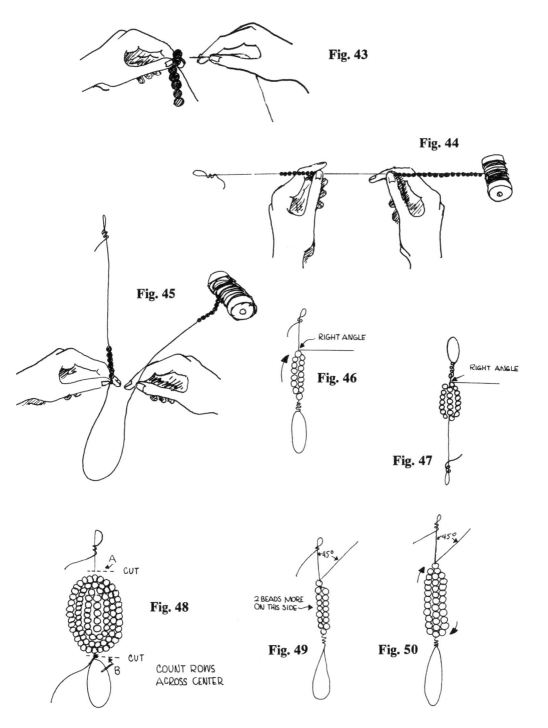

Fig. 43

Fig. 44

Fig. 45

RIGHT ANGLE

Fig. 46

RIGHT ANGLE

Fig. 47

A
CUT
Fig. 48
CUT
B
COUNT ROWS
ACROSS CENTER

45°
2 BEADS MORE
ON THIS SIDE
Fig. 49

45°
Fig. 50

the beads, but for larger loops, measure with a ruler, and be sure to measure accurately.

To make a small center consisting of 5 loops of 10-beads each, put a few inches of beads on the spool or wire, crimp the open end of the wire and move 10 beads to within 4″ of the crimped end of the wire. Make a loop of the 10 beads by folding them in half and twisting the 2 bottom wires together, close to the base of the loop. Twist the wires together, twice, tightly. Close to the base of this first loop, and to the left of it, form another 10-bead loop, and give the beads at least one full twist, thus crossing the wires at the base of the second loop. It makes no difference whether the twist is toward you or away from you, just be consistent with your directions. Most right-handed people make each new loop to the left of the preceding one, but if it is easier for you to make them on the right, do so, as the end result will be the same. Continue, and close to the base of the 2nd loop, make a 3rd. Continue until you have made 5 consecutive 10-bead loops. Allow 4″ of bare wire and cut the wire from the spool. Twist the wires close together under the center of the 5 loops, and swing the loops into a circle. This can be a tiny flower or a center for a larger one. *Fig. 51.*

Continuous Wraparound Loops

Wraparound petals and parts are made the same way as the single loops, except that each small loop of beads is encircled with a row of beads around the outside edge, giving it a double row of beads. Make the same center as before, but wrap around each loop of beads with a row of beads as you work. String more beads on the spool of wire, crimp the open end of the wire, and move 10 beads to within 4″ of the crimped end of the wire. Make a loop of the 10 beads, close it by turning the loop, thus crossing the wires at the bottom of the loop, then wrap around the outside rim of the loop with a row of beads. Wrap bare spool wire, once around the beginning wire at the base of the double loop of beads. Next to this first wrapped loop of beads, but not quite as close as for the single loops, make a second 10-bead loop. Give the loop of beads one full twist to cross the wires at the bottom, and encircle the second loop of beads with a row of beads. Wrap bare spool wire around the base of the second loop, once, to secure the wrapped row of beads. Execute the 3rd, 4th,

108

and 5th loops in the same manner, taking care to wrap bare spool wire around the base of each petal after the original 10-bead loop has been encircled with beads. Allow 4″ of bare spool wire and cut the wire from the spool. *Fig. 52*. The large poppies shown in *Color Plate No. VII* has this technique in one of its center units.

Continuous Crossover Loops

Parts made with the crossover method are basically the same as the continuous single loops, except that each loop has a row of beading either up the front and down the back (for a four row crossover) or a row of beading up the front and bare wire down the back of the loop (for a 3 row crossover). The initial loops should be measured with a ruler for uniformity of size. String at least 24″ of beads, crimp the open end of the spool wire, and move 1½″ of beads to within 4″ of the crimped end of the wire. Form a narrow loop of beads with the 1½″ of beads and tightly twist the wires at the base of the loop twice. Bring the beaded wire up the front of the narrow loop, using just enough beads to fill in the center of the loop. Push excess beads away, so that the bare spool wire crosses over the top of the loop and goes between the beads at the top of the loop. Bring bare spool wire down the back of the loop, and flatten the petal in the middle so that all 3 rows of beads are visible. *Fig. 53*. Wrap bare spool wire around the single wire at the base of the petal. You have just made one 3-row crossover petal. Close to the base of this first petal, form a loop with another 1½″ of beads, give the loop of beads one full twist to cross the wires at the base of the loop, and keeping the loop narrow, bead up the front, then bring bare wire down the back of the loop. Secure the crossover row of beads by wrapping bare spool wire around the base of the 2nd loop, thus securing the crossover row of beads. Continue in this manner until you have made 5 more petals, allow 4″ of bare spool wire and cut the wire from the spool.

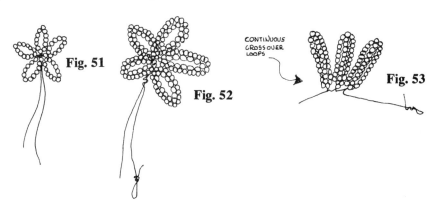

Fig. 51

Fig. 52

CONTINUOUS CROSSOVER LOOPS

Fig. 53

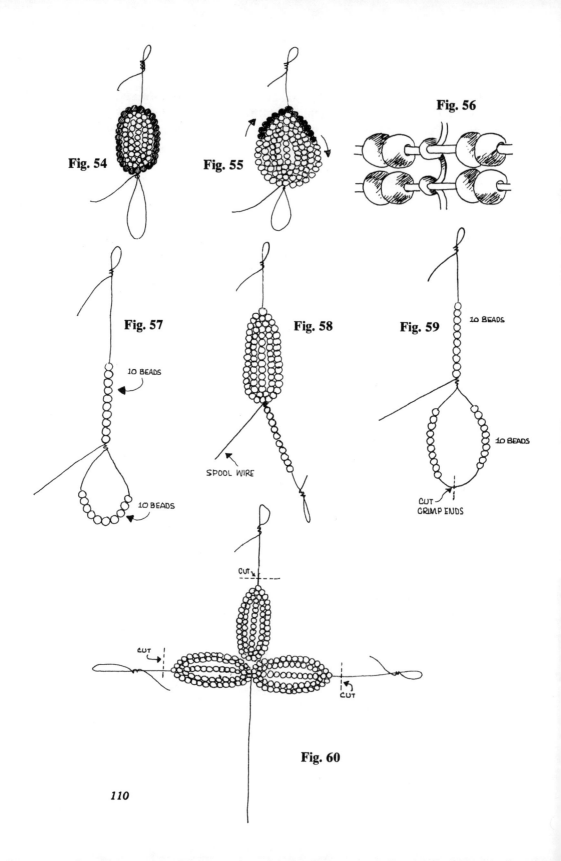

Fig. 54

Fig. 55

Fig. 56

Fig. 57

10 BEADS

10 BEADS

Fig. 58

SPOOL WIRE

Fig. 59

10 BEADS

10 BEADS

CUT
CRIMP ENDS

CUT

CUT

CUT

Fig. 60

Twist the 2 wires together on the underside and in the center of the loops to form a stem, add the single loop unit you made in the center and you will have a charming little daisy. The leaves in the large poppy arrangement are made using this technique.

Shading of Petals

If you wish to shade any of your petals, leave enough bare wire on the petal to completely finish it, as contrasting colors must be fed onto the open end of the wire. For example: make a round petal with a 5 bead basic and 7 rows. Work the 5 bead basic and the first 5 rows in the first color. Measure enough wire to finish the next 2 rows, allow an extra 4" of wire and cut the wire from the spool. Feed on enough beads in a contrasting color to work the 6th and 7th rows and twist the bottom wires together. Tipping a petal is done in the same way. Very attractive effects can be had with shading and tipping. *Figs. 54* and *55*.

Lacing

Lacing is the method used for reinforcing large petals and leaves and joining a series of petals or leaves to one another. To reinforce a single petal or leaf, always start the lacing wire in the middle of the unit, and lace from the center out, on both sides. Cut a piece of 32-gauge wire about 3 times as long as the width of the units to be laced. Straddle the middle of the basic row of beads with the lacing wire. Make sure the right side of the unit is facing up, unless otherwise instructed. Cross the assembly wires over one another, on the wrong side of the unit, to lock them in position. You will be back-stitching from the center row to the outside row, working one side of the unit at a time. *Fig. 56*. Keep the top of the unit to the left. Using the end of the lacing wire that is pointing away from you, bring it under the row of beads next to the basic row (the third row), up between the 3rd and 5th rows, across the top of the 3rd row, and down in front of the 3rd row. Bring the wire under the 3rd row and the 5th row, up in back of the 5th row, across the top of the 5th row, and down in front of the 5th row; under the 5th and 7th rows, up in back of the 7th row, across the top of the 7th row and down in front of the 7th row, etc. until the outer row has been reached. Lace the outer row too, going around the outer row twice to secure the wire. Clip the excess wire away, close to the beads. Reverse your work so that the bottom of the unit is to the left, still right side up, and lace the other side of the unit in the same way.

When joining petals or leaves, one to the other, start the lacing in the middle of the first unit, straddling the basic row of beads, and leave 3″ of the lacing wire pointing away from you. Have the longer wire toward you and cross the wires over in the back. The wires will have reversed their positions, and the shorter wire will be toward you and the longer wire will be pointing away from you. Using the longer end of the wire, lace to the outside row of the petal, and wrap only once around the last row. Place the second unit close to the first one, and on top of the lacing wire, making sure the tops of the units are even. Bring the lacing under, over and down in front of the first row of beads of the second petal, and continue lacing to the other side of the unit. Add the remaining units to be laced together. Turn your work around, still right side up, and lace the other half of the first unit with the short piece of wire. Try to keep the lacing wire in as straight a line as possible.

Beaded Stems

You may bead a flower stem in two ways. The larger flower stems should be wrapped with small beads that have been strung onto a spool of 32-gauge wire, but most small and medium flower stems can be beaded by using large green stem beads.

For wrapped beaded stems, string the small regular 11° beads onto a spool of lacing wire. String at least 3 strands, as most stems require that much. Other longer ones will take more. Wrap the open end of the beaded wire around the base of the flower 3 or 4 times to secure. Push beads up to the stem, and wrap beaded wire around and down the stem to the desired length. Push away any excess beads that are on the wire, wrap bare wire around the stem several times to secure, and cut away any excess lacing wire. Cover the exposed wire with tape.

When using the large stem beads, use 19-gauge wire for the stems of the flowers. Always hook the untaped wire into the wires at the base of the flower to be stemmed. The hook should not exceed ¾″

in length. Secure the hook with a small piece of floral tape. Cover the taped portion with small green beads that have been strung on the lacing wire, cut away all petal wires that hang below the tape, wrap bare lacing wire around the 19-gauge wire at the base of the beading, 2 or 3 times, and cut away the excess very close to the beads. Transfer the desired amount of the large stem beads (3, 4 or 5"), onto the open end of the stem wire. Turn the stem upside down, cover the bare stem wire with tape, and starting the taping from the open end of the stem, tape to the stem beads, including the last two stem beads in the taping. Press the tape firmly to prevent the stem beads from slipping and the stem from turning.

Assembly of Units and Use of Floral Tape

All bare wires at the base of the leaves and all flower stems, (not individual petals) should be covered with tape before adding leaves and flowers to master stems. Tape the heavy stem wires, too. Tear 15 or 20" of tape from its roll and stretch it as far as possible. Always stretch the tape before using. It will be thinner and your stems will be slimmer. The tape is slightly adhesive and it has no right or wrong side. Attach one end of the tape to the base of the leaf flower stems, and wrap around and downward at a bias angle. Press as you wrap. Should you need more tape before the wires are covered, simply add another piece of tape to where you left off, and continue.

Several 6" rulers have been printed at various locations throughout the book for your convenience. When a pattern calls for a specific measurement, it is important that you measure accurately.

Stem Wires

There are several gauge wires used for flower stems. The 12-gauge is very strong, and should be used for all very large flowers with long stems. A 14-gauge wire is still strong enough to hold a very large flower if its stem is going to be short, 12 or 14 inches, for example. The 16-gauge wires are used for most large and medium flowers if the stems are no longer than 14". If the heavier wires are not available to you, you can always combine 2, 3 or 4 pieces of 16-gauge wire for extra strength by taping them together. Wire clothes hangers can be straightened with heavy duty pliers, then cut to desired lengths as they have great strength.

Reducing Wires

There is a standard rule for eliminating bottom wires on petals and leaves. Normally, it isn't necessary to reduce them on leaves, as most leaves, when added to flower stems, do show a bit of stem. Therefor if the basic loop wire is cut open at the bottom of the loop you will have 3 wires.

Petal wires should be reduced to 2 wires and the safest way to do it, is to cut open one side of the basic loop close to the base of the petal, thus allowing the basic loop to become one wire. The second wire is from the spool, and this one should never be cut short, as it could cause a petal to come apart during assembly if the basic wires were to be twisted in the opposite direction. *Fig. 48.*

Split Basic

Because I am constantly trying to find new and better ways to eliminate as many petal wires as possible, the split basic was devised. It eliminates some of the bottom wires without endangering the security of the petal. The end result is a smoother, leaner flower stem.

Single Split Basic

To practice, let's work on a 6-petal daisy with a single split basic. Using a generous basic loop, create a basic of 10 beads, and slip 10 beads more into the basic loop. *Fig. 57.* Make a 5-row petal with a pointed top and round bottom. If the basic loop wires are twisted below the base of the petal, untwist them back to the base of the petal. Push the 10 beads that are in the basic loop to one side of the loop and cut open the basic loop at the bottom. Crimp the open end of the side that has the 10 beads. *Fig. 58.* Wrap the bare spool wire at the base of the 10 beads and using these 10 beads as another basic, make another 5-row petal with a pointed top and round bottom. Wrap bare spool wire twice around the base of the second petal to secure, allow 3″ of bare spool wire and cut the wire from the spool. You will finish with two wires; one wire from the spool and one that is the other half of the original basic loop. Trim off the top basic wires normally. This constitutes one pair of petals.

Make 2 more pairs in the same way, stack all 3 pairs, one on top of the other, bottoms even, and twist the bottom wires together to form a stem. Swing the petals into a circle, curving each petal up and out to shape them. You now only have 6 wires in the flower stem instead of the usual 12.

Double Split Basic

The same 6-petal flower can be made with 1 remaining wire for each 3 petals. Create the same basic of 10 beads, and slip 20 beads into a generous basic loop. Make a 5-row petal with the top 10-bead basic, untwist the basic loop back to the base of the petal, turn the petal upside down, and put 10 beads on each side of the basic loop. *Fig. 59*.

Cut open the basic loop in the middle, crimp both open ends of the wires to prevent the beads from slipping off, wrap bare spool wires twice around the bottom of the 10 basic beads on the left wire, and make a 5-row petal, pointed top, round bottom. Wrap bare spool wire around the base of the 10 beads on the right wire, and make a third 5-row petal. At the completion of the 5th row on the last petal, wrap bare spool wire twice around the base of the third petal to secure. Allow 3″ of bare spool wire and cut the wire from the spool. You now have 3 petals and one wire. *Fig. 60*. Make another set of 3 petals in the same way, stack them, bottoms even, right sides up, and twist the two bottom wires together to form a stem. Shape the petals into a flower.

Flowers with more than 5 rows of beads on their petals can be made in the same way, but more than 2 wraps of wire will be neces- sary at the start of each new petal so that there will be enough space between the base of the first petal and the base of each new petal. You must allow enough space for the rows of beads on each new petal. The space should be equal to the distance between the bottom basic bead of the first petal to the bottom of the bottom row of the first petal.

To make a 5-petal flower, work one pair of petals with a single split basic, and a trio of petals with a double split basic. You will have only 3 wires for the 5 petals. Combine the petals in the same way.

Reverse Wrap

Often, a reverse wrap can give your petals and leaves a neater appear- ance. For example, the front petals of the snapdragon are reverse wrapped at the bottom. This will allow you to hide the wrong side of the bottom of the petal on the inside of the flower, and expose the right side of the top. To reverse wrap, cross the spool wires under and around the bottom basic loop instead of over the top in the usual way. Start the reverse wrap at the end of the 3rd row, and reverse wrap at the completion of every odd numbered row. This will give your petal a right side at the top and a wrong side at the bottom. Whenever a reverse wrap is requested in a pattern, execute it at the round end of the unit, as it is easier, and you will not risk spoiling your point at the other end. If the pattern calls for a round top and round bottom, then it makes no difference which end has the reverse wrap.

DAISY JACKET

Add glamour to a simple evening gown or jump suit. It takes 122 daisies to make a size 10-12 jacket in this design and they are all joined together with gold jump rings to form the pattern.

Materials

> 6½ bunches of pearl beads
> 15 strands of real-gold-lined beads
> 140 gold jump rings
> 26-gauge gold spool wire

Flower

Transfer several strands of pearl beads to a spool of 26-gauge gold wire and 2″ from the open end of the wire make 7 continuous beaded loops, measuring 1½″ of beads for each loop. Allow 2″ of bare wire at the completion of the 7th loop and cut the wire from the spool. Twist both wires together close to the circle of loops. Make 122.

Stamen

Basic: 2 beads, round tops, round bottoms, 6 rows.

The stamen is a small beehive, so it will be mounded. Use 4 beads for row 2, 5 beads for row 3, 6 beads for row 4, 7 beads for row 5, and 8 beads for row 6. Make the required number of beads fit between the top and bottom basic wires. You will finish at the top basic wire as there is an even number of rows. Set a beehive in the center of each daisy and twist together tightly for 1″ the wires of both flower and stamen. Cut away all but ¼″ of the twisted wires, and with a sharp nosed jewelers' pliers, coil the wires and tuck them up into the wrong side of the hollow beehive. Be sure to point the open ends of the wires into the beehive. Otherwise they will have a tendency to pick the fabric of your gown when you wear the jacket.

Assembly

Back

(54 daisies.) Join a row of 9 daisies with a jump ring between each daisy. Make 5 more rows of 9 daisies in the same way and join them to form a section that measures 9 daisies wide and 6 rows long. At the bottom of rows 1, 3, 5, 7 and 9 attach 2 more daisies. *Fig. 61 (1, 3, 5, 7 and 9).*

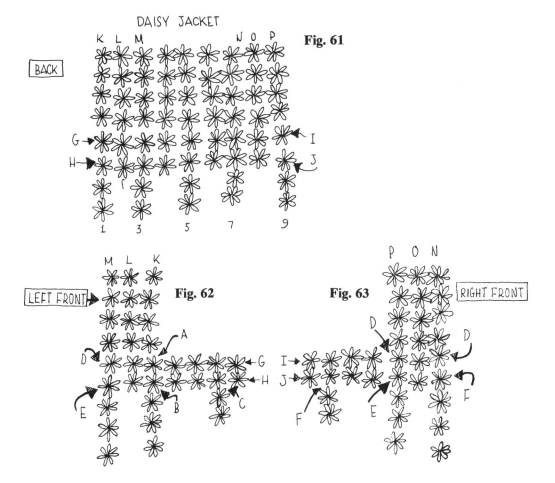

DAISY JACKET

Fig. 61

BACK

Fig. 62

LEFT FRONT

Fig. 63

RIGHT FRONT

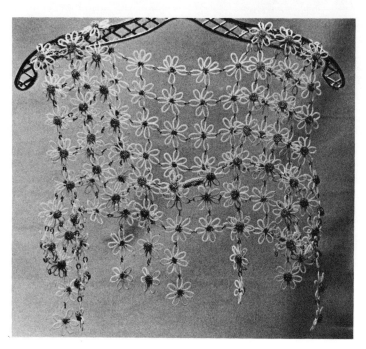

Left Front

(24 daisies.) Make 2 rows of 9 daisies each, and 1 row of 6 daisies and join them with jump rings as in *Fig. 62.*

Underarm

(10 daisies.) At points *(A)* and *(B)* in *Fig. 62* join 2 rows of 4 daisies each and at *(C)* add 2 more.

Right Front

(24 daisies.) Repeat the pattern for the left front to make the right front and add the 10 daisies for the underarm section. With jump rings, join the left front to the left side of the back at points *(G)* and *(H) Fig. 63,* and the right front to the right side of the back at points *(I)* and *(J) Fig. 63.* Join the top of the left front to the top left of the back at points *(K), (L)* and *(M), Fig. 63,* to close the shoulders.

One word of caution; be sure all of the daisies face one direction, right sides up, as you assemble. If you would like the jacket to have a front closing, make 2 more daisies and attach 1 to each side of the front. To one add a jump ring, and to the other, attach a spring ring to catch a ring on the daisy on the opposite side.

DAISY CHOKER ON BLACK VELVET RIBBON

This choker can, of course, be made in any color combination that will coordinate well with your attire. It is shown with black velvet ribbon, and the flower has been worked in pearl beads with gold centers.

Materials

16" of black velvet ribbon, 1½" wide
3 strands pearl beads
1 strand real-gold-lined beads
26-gauge gold spool wire

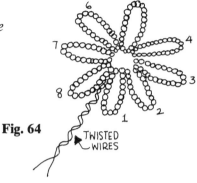

Fig. 64

Daisy

Two inches from the open end of the spool wire make 8 continuous beaded loops, measuring 1¼" of beads for each loop. Allow 2" of bare spool wire at the completion of the last loop and cut the wire from the spool. *Fig. 64.* Balance the wires by bringing the finish wire under loop 1, up between loops 1 and 2, over the base of loop 2, down between loops 2 and 3, under the base of loop 3, up between loops 3 and 4, and down between loops 4 and 5. Join the 2 end wires in the center of the wrong side of the flower and twist them tightly for ½". Make 7.

Centers

This is a small beehive so follow exactly the count for the number of beads for each row, and the center will then be slightly mounded in shape. Make 7 in gold.

Basic: 2 beads, round top, round bottom, 6 rows.

Two inches from the open end of the beaded spool wire, create a basic with 2 beads. Use 4 beads for row 2, 5 beads for row 3, 6 beads for row 4, 7 beads for row 5, and 8 beads for row 6. You will finish at the single basic wire because there are an even number of rows. Cut open the basic loop at the bottom of the loop. Straddle the 2 sets of wires over the center of the daisy so that they protrude through

to the back of the daisy. Twist the wires together tightly for 1", and cut off all but ¼" of the twisted wires. With a sharp-nosed jewelers' pliers tuck the wires all the way into the hollow center of the flower. Find the center of the velvet ribbon and sew on 1 daisy, catching only the outer edges of the petals. Sew 3 to the left and 3 to the right of the center daisy, spacing the flowers so that they just touch one another, not overlap. Sew either 2 snaps or 2 hooks-and-eyes to the outer ends of the ribbon to fasten. Or, if you wish, instant self-cling tape may be sewn to the ends of the ribbon. This will give you an overlapped closing.

SMALL DAISY NECKLACE

For a smaller person, this pink daisy necklace is in better proportion. The ribbon is narrower, and there are 4 smaller daisies with 1 large one in the center.

Materials

    3 strands pink beads
    1 strand gold beads
    14" pink velvet ribbon, 1" width
    26-gauge gold spool wire

Large Daisy

Two inches from the open end of the beaded spool wire make 8 continuous beaded loops, measuring 1¼" of beads for each loop. Balance the wires and twist both wires together in the center of the wrong side of the daisy. Make 1 in pink.

Small Daisy

Two inches from the open end of the beaded wire make 8 continuous beaded loops, measuring 1" of beads for each loop. Balance the wires and twist them together in the center of the wrong side of the daisy. Make 4 in pink.

Centers

Basic: 2 beads, round tops, round bottoms, 10 rows.
Use the same count and method as for the centers in the pearl daisy choker on black velvet. Make 5 in gold.

Assembly

Sew the large daisy in the center of the ribbon and 2 smaller ones on each side, catching only the outer edge of each petal. Close the same as the black velvet choker.

DAISY CHAIN NECKLACE

For the ultimate in daintiness, the daisy chain necklace without the velvet ribbon under it, is the answer. Although it uses jewelry findings for assembling, the flowers are worked on wire, as usual, and the pattern is the same as for those used on the black velvet choker.

Materials

4 strands of pearl beads
2 strands real-gold-lined beads
26-gauge gold spool wire
9 small gold jump rings
1 gold spring ring

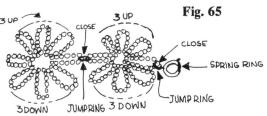

Fig. 65

Flowers

Make 8 continuous beaded loops, measuring 1¼″ of beads for each loop. Make 8 in pearl.

Centers

Basic: 2 beads, round tops, round bottoms, 6 rows, **mounded.**
Make 8 in gold.

Assembly of Flower

Straddle the wires of the centers across the daisy loops, bring them to the back of the daisy and twist them together tightly for 1″. Cut off all but ¼″ of the twisted wires and bend them up into the hollow center of the flower.

Assembly of Necklace

Using either 2 sharp-nosed jewelers' pliers or one plier and a pointed tweezer for your working tools, open a gold jump ring and hook 1 end of it into the small loop on the gold spring ring. To the other end attach the outer edge of 1 loop of 1 daisy. Reclose the jump ring with the pliers. Open another jump ring and hook it into the beaded loop directly opposite the first jump ring, and attach another daisy onto the same ring. Close the ring with the pliers. Join 9 daisies, and be sure to link them right side up so that there are 3 beaded loops up and 3 down as in *Fig. 65*. Add a jump ring to the outside of the 9th daisy, and close the ring. This one will be used for the spring ring to close the necklace. This same necklace can be shortened to 5 flowers and assembled in the same way, thus making it into a bracelet to match the necklace.

PEARL DAISY BELT ON BLACK VELVET RIBBON

The number of pearl daisies is optional, depending on whether or not you wish them to be all around. There are 9 daisies on the belt shown and they cover the front half of the belt only.

Materials

5 strands of beads for flowers
2 strands of beads for centers
32″ velvet ribbon, 1½″ wide
26-gauge gold spool wire

Flowers

The daisy size is the same as for the daisy choker on black velvet and they are sewn on in the same way. Choose either snaps, hooks-and-eyes or instant self-cling tape for closing. Make 9.

DAISY EARRINGS

The smaller size daisy makes a more attractive earring. Create a pair to match a choker and belt.

Materials

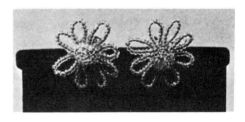

    1 strand of beads for flowers
    ½ strand of beads for centers
    26-gauge gold spool wire
    2 perforated disc earring backs in gold

Flowers

Using the same count as for the small daisy shown on the pink choker, make 2.

Centers

Using the same count as for the daisy choker, make 2 in a contrasting color.

Assembly

Combine the loops and the center the same as for the daisies on the chokers, and attach the flowers to the perforated discs the same as for the primrose earrings in this chapter.

ORANGE BLOSSOM NECKLACE

An orange blossom is the perfect choice for the petite June bride. These flowers are made with continuous wraparound loops.

Fig. 66

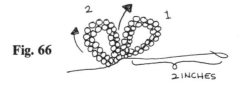

Materials

> 5 strands of pearl beads
> 2 strands of real-gold-lined beads
> 26-gauge gold spool wire
> 1 gold spring ring
> 9 gold jump rings

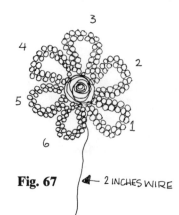

Fig. 67   2 INCHES WIRE

Flowers

Two inches from the open end of the beaded spool wire make a pear shaped beaded loop wtih 15 beads. Wrap the beaded wire around the outside edge of the beaded loop and secure by wrapping bare spool wire once around the bottom of the double beaded loop. To the left, and close to the first double loop, make another 15 bead loop and wrap around it with a row of beads. *Fig. 66.* Continue until you have 6 double beaded loops. Allow 2″ of bare wire and cut the wire from the spool. *Fig. 67.* Make 8 in pearl.

Centers

Basic: 2 beads, round tops, round bottoms, 10 rows, the same as for daisy. Make 8 in gold, mounded.

Assembly

Place a center in the middle of each flower and twist both sets of wires together tightly on the underside of the flower. Cut away all but ¼″ of the twisted wires and turn the twisted wires up into the hollow beehive center with jeweler's pliers. Join the orange blossoms with gold jump rings and a spring ring, the same as for the daisy necklace. Five of these flowers will make a bracelet to match the necklace, and 2 can be attached to gold earring backs for a pair.

BEEHIVE EARRINGS

These earrings can be easily worked with 2- or 3-color combinations, or all in one shade. If you follow the bead count for each row, and make them fit between the top and bottom wires, the beehive will automatically form.

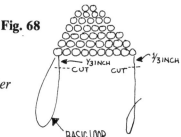

Fig. 68

Materials

   2 strands of beads
   26-gauge gold spool wire
   2 perforated disc earring backs, ⅝" in diameter

Beehive

Basic: 2 beads, round tops, round bottoms, 14 rows.
Four inches from the open end of the beaded spool wire, create a basic of 2 beads, leaving a generous basic loop of bare wire (8"). For row 2 use 4 beads; row 3, 5 beads; row 4, 6 beads; row 5, 7 beads; row 6, 8 beads; row 7, 9 beads; row 8, 10 beads; row 9, 11 beads; row 10, 12 beads; row 11, 13 beads; row 12, 14 beads; row 13, 15 beads; and row 14, 16 beads. The 14 rows should build the beehive so that the diameter of the opening equals ⅝", which is the same as the perforated earring disc. If it does not, increase a row or two until it does. Reduce the basic loop to 2 wires by cutting the loop open on one side, leaving ⅓" on the one side. Cut away the spool wire, leaving only ⅓". *Fig. 68.* Push these 2 short wires into the beehive, and use the 2 longer wires to attach the beehive to the disc by inserting them into 2 opposite holes of the disc, from front to back, *Fig. 69 (A)* and *(B)* and wrapping them twice through each hole. Cut off excess wires close to the disc. Make 2.

To make a 2-color beehive, work the basic and the next 7 rows in one color, allow 15" of bare spool wire, cut the wire from the spool, and feed on enough beads in a contrasting color to work the remaining rows. To make a 3-color beehive, work the basic and the next 5 rows in color No. 1, allow 20" of bare spool wire and cut the wire

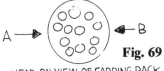
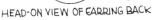

A → B

Fig. 69

HEAD-ON VIEW OF EARRING BACK

from the spool. Feed on enough beads in color No. 2 to work rows 7, 8, 9 and 10, then feed on enough beads in color No. 3 to finish the remaining rows.

CUFF LINKS

Shirtwaist fashions are in again, and should your blouse have French cuffs that are in need of cuff links, you can make your own in colors to match.

Fig. 70

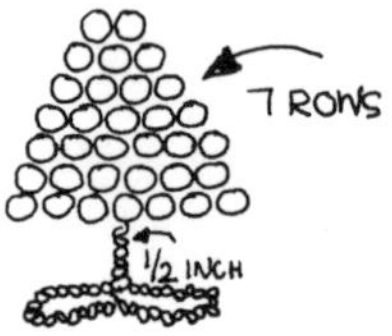

Materials

   2 strands of beads
   26-gauge gold spool wire

Using the pattern for the beehive earrings, leave 5″ of bare wire on the top basic and work with at least 10″ of bare wire in the bottom basic loop; and make a beehive in the colors of your choice. Cut open the basic loop at the bottom of the loop. Bring both top basic wire and bottom loop wires together in the center of the opening of the beehive and twist them together for 3″. Cut away any wires that extend beyond 3″. One-half-inch beyond the base of the beehive form the twisted wires into a narrow horizontal loop, *Fig. 70,* using ½″ for each loop. Twist the 2 side loops together and twist the remaining twisted wires around the ½″ of twisted wires at the base of the beehive. Either trim away or tuck into the beehive the excess twisted wires.

PRIMROSE EARRINGS

Have earrings to match every ensemble. They can be made in solid colors or 2- and 3-color combinations because there are 3 units to each. Do them all in one color first.

Materials

   3 strands of 11° beads
   26-gauge gold spool wire
   1 pair perforated earring backs

Fig. 71

Fig. 72

Unit 1

Four inches from the open end of the spool wire, make 4 continuous loops of beads using 10 beads for each loop. Allow 4″ of bare wire and cut the wire from the spool. *Fig. 71. Make one for each earring.*

Unit 2

Four inches from the open end of the wire, make a 10 bead loop and wrap a row of beads around the outside edge, creating a double loop. Repeat 3 more times, all on one wire, for a 4-petal unit. Leave 4″ of bare spool wire and cut the wire from the spool. *Fig. 72. Make one for each earring.*

Fig. 73

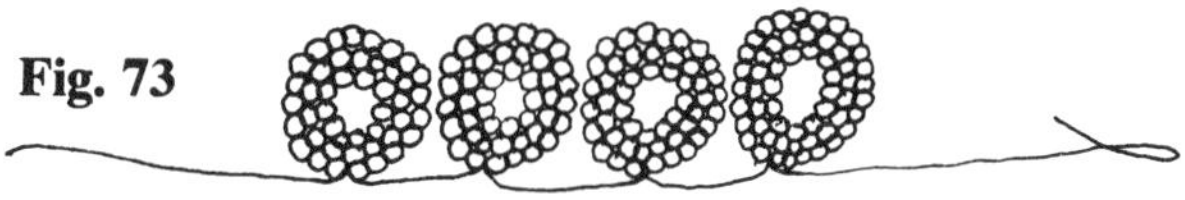

Unit 3

Four inches from the open end of the wire, make a 10-bead loop, wrap beaded wire around it twice, creating a triple loop. Repeat 3 more times, all on one wire, for a 4 petal unit. Leave 4″ of bare wire and cut the wire from the spool. *Fig. 73. Make one for each earring.*

Assembly

Set one unit 1 on top of one unit 2 so that the loops match, and twist together both sets of wires for no more than ¼″ Set the combined units 1 and 2 on top of one unit 3 so that the loops match, and twist all wires together tightly all the way. Cut away the last ½″ of wires so that there are no loose ends. Crush the loops upward to give the flower its shape. Insert the twisted wires of the flower into the center hole of one earring back, from front to back. *Fig. 74 (A)* pulling them tightly until the back of the flower rests firmly onto the perforated disc. Bring the twisted wires down the back of the perforated disc, and wrap them tightly several times around the earring frame at the bottom of the disc. *Fig. 74 (B).* Cut away the excess wires and flatten the ends with a pliers. For a 2-color combination, work units 1 and 3 in one shade and unit 2 in a contrast. For a 3-color combination, make each unit a different shade.

Here is a measurement guide for each unit so that you can put to good use some of your leftover strands of beads. Unit 1 uses 2½″ of beads (5″ for a pair), unit 2 uses 6″ (12″ for a pair), and unit 3 takes 14″ (28″ for a pair).

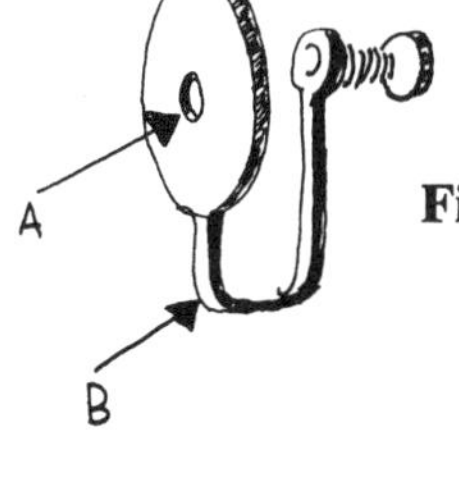

A

Fig. 74

B

127

STRAWBERRY KEY CHAIN

There's only one color for this one because it really looks best in red. But you can use red transparent, irridescent or opaque beads.

Materials

1 strand each of red and green beads
26-gauge gold spool wire
1 gold-plated key chain

Berry

Basic: 2 beads, round tops, round bottoms, 26 rows.

Four inches from the open end of the spool wire, create a basic with 2 beads, and work with a generous basic loop of wire. Follow the pattern, using the exact number of beads given for each row, and your strawberry will automatically form itself. Row 2, 4 beads; row 3, 5 beads; row 4, 6 beads; row 5, 7 beads; row 6, 8 beads; row 7, 9 beads; row 8, 10 beads; row 9, 11 beads; row 10, 12 beads; row 11, 13 beads; row 12, 14 beads; row 13, 15 beads; row 14, 16 beads; row 15, 16 beads; rows 16 through 21, 17 beads, rows 22 and 23, 16 beads; and rows 24 through 26, 14 beads. At the completion of the 3rd row, bend both top and bottom wires down. *Fig. 75.* As you progress you will actually be working around the tip of the forefinger of your left hand. You will finish the 26th row at the single basic wire, as there are an even number of rows. Note: There are 13 rows of beads on one side of the basic 2 beads, and 12 rows on the other side; 25 rows plus the basic is 26 rows. Combine both sets of wires in the center opening at the top of the berry, and twist them for ½". Make 1 in red.

Calyx

Four inches from the open end of the spool wire make 5 continuous 3-row crossover loops, measuring 1" of beads for each initial loop. Keep the initial loop narrow. *(see Methods section for crossover technique Fig. 53).* Make 1 in green.

13 ROWS

Fig. 75

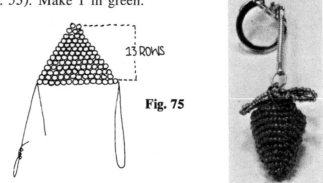

Assembly

Add the calyx to the top of the berry by placing it with its wrong side next to the berry. Bend the crossover loops down over the top of the berry and twist both berry and calyx wires together all the way. Attach the wires to the key ring in the usual way, cut off excess wires and flatten the open ends of the wires with a jeweler's pliers.

BEADED BALL KEY RING

These are a quick and easy fun gift for a hostess, or door prize. Great for fund raising, too.

Materials

1 cork ball, 1¼″ in diameter
2 strands 11° beads
12″ of gold spool wire 26-gauge
1 gold-plated key ring
White glue, and small paintbrush

Center Stem

Transfer about 12 beads to the gold wire and 5″ from the open end of the wire create a basic of 2 beads, giving it a row of beads on each side, round top, round bottom. Cut open the bottom basic wire at the bottom of the loop, and twist together the both sets of wires in the center of the wrong side of the 3 row unit. Twist tightly for 4″ and cut the wire from the spool.

Beading the Ball

Gently remove 1 strand of beads from the bunch and knot 1 end, slipping 1 bead into the knot as you make it. Use as little thread as possible for the knot. Dip the beaded knot into a bit of the glue and insert the glued knot into 1 hole of the cork ball. Insert the twisted gold wires of the center stem into the same hole, pulling it all the way through the ball so that it rests flat against it covering the hole. With a small paintbrush, spread glue on ⅓ of the ball, around the center unit. Using the beads on the thread, glue 2 or 3 rows of beads around the ball, keeping the beads and the rows of beads close together. Add another band of glue and add another 2 or 3 rows of beads, but let each few rows "set" for a minute or two before proceeding. This will give the glue a chance to dry a bit. Keep the fingers free of glue with a slightly moistened cloth. When one strand of beads has been added, leave ¼″ of bare thread and secure it with glue, cutting away the excess thread. Start a second strand close to the last bead of the 1st strand, and continue gluing this strand of beads around the ball. Leave ¼″ of bare thread, secure it with glue, and cut away any excess thread when the glue is completely dry. Attach the beaded ball to the small ring on a key chain the same way as for the flower chain. If you want a smaller ball, ¾″ cork balls can be used. One-inch oval corks are also available.

FLOWER KEY CHAIN

No matter when you carry this key chain, it will be a conversation novelty. Make it in white pearl and real gold beads for evening wear, or in colors to coordinate with the interior of your car. Dangling from the dashboard, it will surely add a feminine touch. No more scrounging in the bottom of your purse; it will be easy to find and fun to use.

Materials

    4 strands of 11° beads for petals
    2 strands of green beads for calyx
    ½ strand of yellow beads for center
    1 gold-plated key chain
    26-gauge gold spool wire
    green floral tape

5 ROWS
Fig. 76

Petals

Basic: 4 beads, round tops, pointed bottoms, 9 rows.
Working with a generous basic loop of wire, about 6″; reduce the bottom wires to 2 by cutting open the basic loop on one side close to the bottom of the petal. Leave the top basic wire on, as it will be used later in assembly. Make 8 petals.

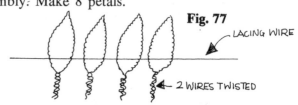
Fig. 77
LACING WIRE
2 WIRES TWISTED

Center

Basic: 2 beads, round top, round bottom, 10 rows.

This is a mounded center like a beehive. Use the following count of beads for each row, and if you make them fit between the top and bottom wires, you will easily create the mounded effect. Working with a generous basic loop and 3″ of top basic wire, create a basic with 2 beads. Use 4 beads for row 2, 5 beads for row 3, 6 beads for row 4, 7 beads for row 5, 8 beads for row 6, 9 beads for row 7, 10 beads for row 8, 11 beads for row 9 and 12 beads for row 10. Starting at the completion of the 3rd row, bend the top and bottom wires down. *Fig. 76.* This will permit the desired number of beads to fit more easily as you work the remaining rows. Because the pattern calls for an even number of rows (10) you will finish at the single wire. Cut open the basic loop at the bottom of the loop. Make 1 in yellow for each flower.

Calyx

Basic: 4 beads, pointed tops, pointed bottoms, 7 rows.

Work with a generous basic loop and reduce the bottom wires to 2 by cutting open one side of the basic loop close to the bottom of the leaf. Trim off the top basic wires on each, leaving only ¼″, and turn it back, as usual, pressing the ¼″ of wire flat against the wrong side of the leaf. Make 4 in green for each flower.

With the right side of the calyx leaves facing up, lace all 4 together with a 10″ piece of the gold spool wire. *Fig. 77.* Fold the 4 leaves in half, wrong sides in, and join them together by twisting the lacing wires together for ⅓″. Cut away all but ¼″ of the twisted wires and tuck them into the wrong side of the combined leaves. Do not combine the bottom wires.

Assembly

Put 2 petals together, one on top of the other, right sides facing each other, and tops even. Twist together tightly the 2 top basic wires for 1″ and cut away all but a ½″. Press the ½″ of wire flat against the wrong side of one petal. Open the 2 petals, wrong sides up, then bring the 2 sets of bottom wires together so that the wrong sides of the petals are facing each other. Twist the bottom basic wires together twice, tightly. This will give you one double-faced petal. Repeat with the 6 remaining petals and you will have 4 double petals. Stack all 4 double petals so that the bottoms are even, and twist the bottom wires together for ½″. If you use a small jeweler's pliers to twist, the wires will have a neater twist. Swing all 4 petals into a circle, then lift each petal up and out to form a trumpet. Between any 2 petals, slide the stamen, and add 1 or 2 wraps of floral tape to hold the wires together. Holding the laced calyx with its wires pointing down, insert the petal wires into the top, and pull them all the way down so that the petals fit snugly into the calyx. Tape the bottom wires securely several times around for ½″ only. Cut away all wires at the base of the tape and cover the open ends with a bit of tape. Transfer 3 or 4 inches of green beads to the gold wire and attach the open end of the wire to the base of one calyx leaf, leaving 3 or 4″ of bare wire. Twist the wires once to secure them and run the piece of bare wire down one side of the taped part of the flower. With beaded wire, cover the taped part of the flower by wrapping the beaded wire around and around until you reach the bottom of the tape. Include the bare starting wire as you wrap. When the tape has been covered, push excess green beads away, twist the 2 end wires together very tightly for 2½″, and cut the wire from the spool. Attach the flower to the key ring by pulling these twisted wires twice through the gold ring at the end of the key chain, then twice around themselves between the ring and the bottom of the green beads. Cut away excess wires and press the ends flat with pliers.

Floral tape comes in many shades, so coordinate the tape color with the bead color when you wrap the base of the flower.

HANGING BASKET

Any miniature flower is a pretty filler for this dainty hanging basket. *Plate No. X* shows buttercups, but the miniature fuchsias are lovely, too. The basket, of course, can be done in any color.

Materials

 1 bunch of green beads
 32-gauge spool wire
 24-gauge spool wire

Basket

Cut 12 pieces of the 24-gauge wire 9″ long. Stack all 12 wires so that they are even at the bottom and twist all 12 of them together, tightly, at one end, for ⅔″. *Fig. 78*. Holding the twisted wires with the untwisted wires pointing upward, arrange the untwisted wires like the spokes of a wheel, horizontally. *Fig. 79*. Make 6 pairs of spokes by twisting every 2 wires together for 2½″. This will form the frame around which the basket is to be made. *Fig. 80*. Transfer 5 strands of green beads onto a spool of 32-gauge wire. Attach the open end of the beaded wire around the ⅔″ piece of the 12 twisted wires by wrapping it 4 or 5 times at the point where the 6 pairs of wires spread out to form the spokes. Select one double wire as a starting point, put a ½″ bend at its outer end. This will make it easier to find the start of each new row of beads as you work. Wrap bare spool wire around the base of this one spoke, wrapping the wire across the top, to the back and over the top again. Between this first spoke and the second one, place two beads, securing them by crossing bare spool wire over the top and around the base of the second spoke. Place 2 beads between the 2nd and 3rd spoke, securing them by wrapping bare spool wire over and around the 3rd spoke. Continue putting 2 beads between each spoke until you have worked 1 row around. *Fig. 81*. For the second row, put 3 beads between each spoke, and for the 3rd row put 4 beads between each spoke. After the 3rd row of beads it will not be necessary to count the number of beads between each spoke. Use whatever amount will fill the space. Keep the spokes evenly spaced and your work flat. Continue filling in the spaces until 10 rows have been completed. *Fig. 82*. At the completion of the 10th row, bend each spoke down sharply so that the spokes are parallel to the twisted wires that are under the

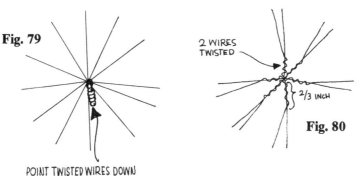

Fig. 79

POINT TWISTED WIRES DOWN

2 WIRES TWISTED

⅔ INCH

Fig. 80

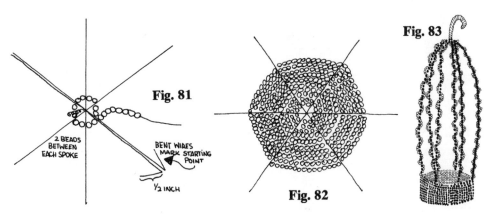

Fig. 81

2 BEADS BETWEEN EACH SPOKE

BENT WIRES MARK STARTING POINT

½ INCH

Fig. 82

Fig. 83

first 10 rows. Work 11 more rows down the sides, and secure the 11th row by wrapping bare spool wire several times around the last spoke, close to the beads, then cut away the excess spool wire. To the double wires of each spoke, transfer 4½″ of beads and secure the beads by twisting each of the 2 wires together. *Fig. 83.* Twist each pair of double beaded wires to spiral the beads. When all spokes have been beaded, spiraled and closed, gather together the top, unbeaded portions of the wires, twist them together and tape them. Wrap this portion of taped wires with green beads that have been strung on 32-gauge wire. Start at the top and wrap to the spokes. End off by wrapping bare 32-gauge wire around the top of 1 spoke several times, then cut off excess wire close to the beads. Bow out the spokes of the cage to give it shape, and bend the top wrapped wires to form a hook.

To prepare the basket for potting, cover a small flat ball of modeling clay with floral tape. If possible, use a tape that is nearly the color of the beads used in the basket, and press the taped clay into the center of the basket. A small piece of styrofoam, cut to fit, can be lightly glued in, if you wish, since the flowers in the basket, being miniature, will not be very heavy.

MINIATURE FRENCH BUTTERCUPS

Field buttercups are yellow, but these are lovely in any pastel. The charming sprigs are made all in one. The flowers are not added to the greenery but are created as you work. In the hanging basket in *Color Plate X* there are several sprigs of buttercups, and the flowers have been combined with the pattern worked just in green. To every sprig with flowers there are 2 plain green ones.

Fig. 84

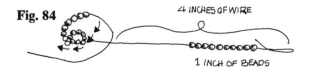

4 INCHES OF WIRE

1 INCH OF BEADS

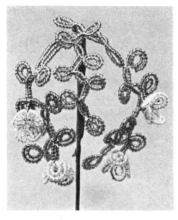

Materials

(for 1 cluster of 2 green sprigs and 1 with flower)

3 strands green beads
2 strands white beads
26-gauge gold spool wire

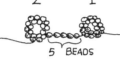

Fig. 85

5 BEADS   1 INCH

All-Green Sprig

To become familiar with the pattern, let's do 1 all-green sprig first. Transfer 1 strand of green beads to a spool of 26-gauge gold wire and crimp the open end of the wire. Measure 1″ of beads and push them to the crimped end of the wire. Four inches from the crimped end of the wire count off 8 more beads and form them into a circle, closing the circle of beads with 1 full twist of the wires close to the base of the circle of 8 beads. Wrap beaded wire once around the outer edge of the 8-bead circle, closely, to form a double loop. Secure the wraparound by wrapping bare spool wire around the base of the double loop, once. *Fig. 84.* Push 5 beads close to the base of the double loop, make another 8 bead loop with 1 wraparound close to the opposite end of the 5 beads. *Fig. 85.* Continue in this manner until you have made 8 double loops, each 1 separated by 5 beads. *Fig. 86.* Swing the loops, alternately, with every other one to the left and every other one to the right. *Fig. 87.* Push 5 more beads to the base of the 8th loop and wrap bare wire once around the base of the 7th loop. Push 5 beads to the base of the 7th loop and wrap bare spool wire around the base of the 6th loop. Push 5 beads to the base of the 6th loop and wrap bare spool wire around the base of the 5th loop. Continue in this manner until you have 5 more beads between each loop, thus giving each double loop a double row of 5 beads between each of them. *Fig. 88.* After wrapping wire around the bottom loop, measure another 1″ of beads to the first 1″ of beads, push the beads on both of the wires toward the bottom double loop and twist the bottom bare wires together to form a stem.

Sprig with Flower Added

Transfer another strand of green beads to the spool wire and make the 8 double loops all in green, just as you did before. Swing the loops, left and right, as in *Fig. 89*. Bring 5 beads between the 8th and 7th loops and the 7th and 6th loops, push 5 beads to the base of the 6th loop, measure 25″ of bare spool wire and cut the wire from the spool. These last 5 beads will be the first half of the stem of the first buttercup. Onto the open end of the extended 25″ piece of bare wire transfer approximately 6″ of yellow beads. Push 8 yellow beads close to the 5 green ones, make an 8 bead loop with the yellow ones and wrap around the 8 bead loop once, creating 1 petal of the buttercup. Repeat with 3 more double loops in yellow to complete the 4-petal flower. Remove any remaining yellow beads from the wire and feed on 20 green ones. Use 5 green beads for the 2nd half of the stem of the first flower, wrapping bare wire around the bottom of the first 5 green beads. Use the next 10 green beads to create the double rows of beads between the next 2 green double loops. The remaining 5 green beads will be the first half of the stem of the 2nd buttercup. Transfer another 6″ of yellow beads to the wire and create another 4-petal buttercup. Feed on approximately 2 more inches of green beads, using 5 for the 2nd half of the stem of the second buttercup and 5 beads each between the remaining 4 green loops, plus 1″ to match the first inch of green. Twist the bottom wires together to form a stem. Shape the flowers by cupping the petals toward the center. This pattern can be lengthened or shortened to suit your individual needs. *Color Plate No. X* shows 8 groupings (4 on each side), and each group has 2 green and 1 with a flower. Each grouping of 3 has been mounted on short pieces of 19-gauge wire for extra support.

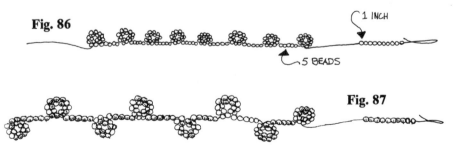

Fig. 86   1 INCH

5 BEADS

Fig. 87

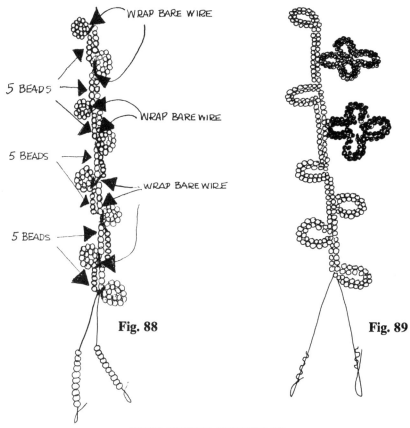

WRAP BARE WIRE

5 BEADS

5 BEADS

WRAP BARE WIRE

5 BEADS

WRAP BARE WIRE

Fig. 88

Fig. 89

MINIATURE FUCHSIAS

This charming miniature can be used in so many ways. Clustered or trailing, mixed with other small flowers, or all by itself as shown in *Color Plate No. X*. The use of gold wire and split basic techniques keep the stems slim and in proportion.

Materials

(for 1 sprig of 3 flowers and leaves)
  1½ strands light(fuchsia beads)
  2¼ strands dark(purple beads)
  2½ strands of light green
  9 black seed beads
  26-gauge gold spool wire
  18- or 19-gauge stem wires for mounting

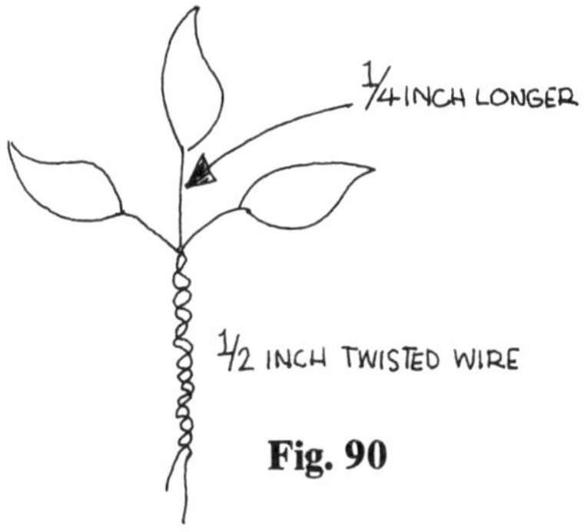

¼ INCH LONGER

½ INCH TWISTED WIRE

Fig. 90

Top Flower Petals

Basic: 5 beads, round tops, round bottoms, 5 rows.

Make the 3 top round petals all in one, by using the double split

137

basic method. (See beginning of this chapter *Fig. 59*). Create a basic of 5 beads and slip 10 beads into a generous basic loop. Build a 5-row petal around the original 5-bead basic, place 5 beads on each side of the basic loop, cut open the bottom of the basic loop, crimp both open ends of the wire to keep from losing the beads, and build a 5-row petal onto each new 5-bead basic. You will finish with 1, wire. Allow 5″ of bare wire and cut the wire from the spool. Repeat for 2 more flowers.

Bottom Flower Petals

Basic: 5 beads, pointed tops, round bottoms, 5 rows.

Make the 4 pointed petals in pairs, this time using the single split basic technique for each pair. Create a basic with 5 beads, slipping 5 beads into a generous basic loop. Make the first 5-row petal; pointed top, round bottom, slide the 5 beads that are in the basic loop to one side of the loop, cut open the loop at the bottom, and build a second 5-row petal onto the 5 beads that have been slipped into the basic loop. You will finish with 2 wires. Repeat for the second pair.

Stamens

Cut 3 pieces of gold wire 6″ long. Into the center of each, place 1 black bead, fold the wire in half and twist 2 of them for 1¼″. Twist the 3rd one for 1½″. Make 3 for each flower in black. Combine the 3 stamens at the bottom of the twisted wires and twist all 3 stamens together for the last ½″.

Leaves

Basic: For small leaves use 5 beads, pointed tops, round bottoms, 3 rows.

Basic: For large leaves use 5 beads, pointed tops, round bottoms, 5 rows.

Work with at least 4″ of bare spool wire in the bottom basic loops, and reduce the bottom wires to 2 by cutting open the basic loop at the base of the leaf. Twist the 2 remaining wires together for 1″. Make 3 small and 1 large, in green, for each flower.

Assembly of Leaves

Combine the small leaves in groups of 3, allowing the center leaf ¼″ more stem than the other two. *Fig. 90.* Twist all 3 sets of wires together for ½″.

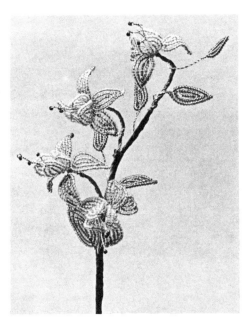

Assembly of Flower

Cup the 3 round petals, wrong sides in, and insert the 3 stamens in the center of the 3 petals. Let the stamens extend ⅔" beyond the tops of the round petals and twist the petal stem wire around the combined stamen wires for ½".

Combine 2 pairs of pointed petals by setting them close together at the bottom, and right sides up. Twist the bottom wires together for ½" very close to the base of the petals. Slide the stems of the combined round petals and stamens between any 2 of the pointed petals and twist all wires together for 1½". Add a set of 3 leaves to the flower stem and twist all wires for ½". Add a large leaf, then twist all wires together all the way to the bottom. Add the leaves alternately, on the right and on the left of the flower stems for variation. Combine 3 flowers and their leaves with 3"or 4" piece of 18- or 19-gauge stem wire to reinforce them.

MINIATURE TURTLES

For a special effect in an arrangement or for just plain fun, try a quaint little turtle resting on a lily pad or display a proud mama turtle taking a stroll with her family of little ones.

Materials

3 strands of green beads
26-gauge gold or silver spool wire

139

Large Turtle—Body

Basic: 6 beads, round tops, round bottoms, 14 rows.

Because you have an even number of rows, you will finish at the top basic wire. Wrap bare spool wire twice tightly around the top basic wire and cut it off close to the basic wire, leaving 1 wire. Reduce the bottom wires to 2 by cutting open the bottom basic loop on 1 side close to the beads. Make 2 in green.

Large Turtle—Head, Legs and Tail

These 3 parts are made all in one. Transfer no less than 10″ of green beads to the spool wire. Four inches from the open end of the wire, make a narrow beaded loop using 15 beads. Bead up the front and down the back of the narrow loop, creating a 4-row crossover unit. Secure the crossover by wrapping bare spool wire once around the wire at the bottom of the unit. This completes the head of the turtle. For the neck, wrap beaded wire 4 times around the wire at the base of the head. This should equal ⅓″. Keep the wrapped beads close together. At the base of the wrapped beading twist both wires together for ¾″. *Fig. 91 (A).* For the pair of front legs make a narrow beaded loop ¾″ out and to the left of the 2 twisted wires, and measure 1½″ of beads for the loop. Twist the two wires together for ¾″, *Fig. 92 (B).* Directly opposite this loop create another one, ¾″ out and to the right, using 1½″ of beads for the 2nd loop. Twist the 2 wires together for ¾″. For the pair of back legs repeat as for the front legs, using the same measurements. Twist both wires together and make a beaded loop with 1″ of beads. Give the beaded loop 1½ turns to cross the wires at the base of the loop and this will make the tail. Allow 2″ of bare spool wire and cut the wire from the spool. *Fig. 93.* Make 1 in green.

Assembly

Join the 2 units of the body by stacking them back to back, right sides facing in and bottoms even. Twist together both sets of bottom wires for ½″, then cut away all but ⅓″. Open the 2 units with the wrong sides facing up. Cup both units so that one is concave and the other convex by pressing your thumbs into the centers of each until they are spoon-shaped. For the concave one, press thumbs into the wrong side. For the convex one, press thumbs into the center of the right side. With the concave unit facing up, set Unit 2 on top. Secure the head by wrapping the top basic wire around the base of the neck. Fold the convex unit over the concave one and join them by twisting both top basic wires together for ½″. Cut off all but ¼″ of the twisted wires and tuck them out of sight into the body of the turtle. Pull out the tail at the bottom and secure it by wrapping its extended 2″ piece of wire once between the outer rows of each of the 2 halves of the body. Cut it off short and tuck it into the body of the turtle and out of sight. Give each of the legs and the tail ½ twist in the center of the loops. Bend the legs down so that they will support the turtle. Raise the head and lower the tail.

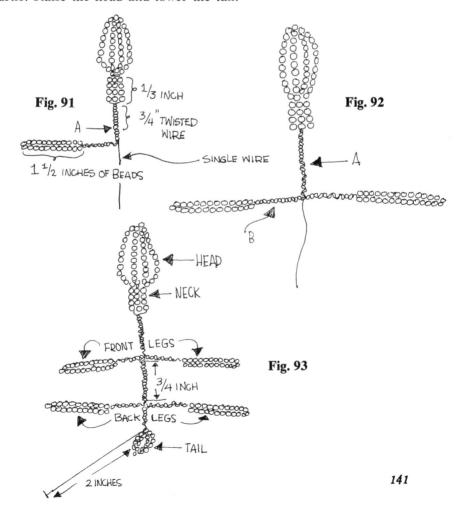

Fig. 91

1/3 INCH

A

3/4″ TWISTED WIRE

SINGLE WIRE

1 ½ INCHES OF BEADS

Fig. 92

A

B

HEAD

NECK

FRONT LEGS

Fig. 93

3/4 INCH

BACK LEGS

TAIL

2 INCHES

Small Turtle—Body

The small turtle is made and assembled in the same way as the larger one, but the measurements are smaller. Make 2.

Basic: 5 beads, round tops, round bottoms, 8 rows.

Head: make a 10-bead narrow loop and bead up the front and down the back. *Neck:* Wrap 2 rows of beads around the bottom wires of the head and twist the 2 wires for ⅜″ instead of ¾″. *Legs:* Use 1″ of beads for each leg and separate all parts by ⅜″ instead of ¾″. *Tail:* Use 12 beads in the loop for the tail .

Assembly

Shape and combine the same as for the larger turtle.

PUMPKIN

Materials

> 5 bunches orange beads
> 4 strands medium green beads
> 26-gauge silver spool wire
> 26 or 27-gauge gold spool wire
> 7½″ of 16-gauge stem wire

Sections

Basic: 5 inches, pointed tops, round bottoms, 19 rows.

Because these sections are so large and can become a bit unruly, may I suggest that you lace them, individually, with the gold wire as you make them. Make 9 in orange. Work the first 7 rows, then lace in 3 places, once through the middle, 10 basic beads down from the top and 10 basic beads up from the bottom. Lace with the right side facing up. Ten inches of gold wire for each lacing will be sufficient.

Work 3 or 4 rows on each side and lace them, 3 or 4 more rows, then lace, until you have completed all 19 rows. Make the top basic wire extra long and work with at least 12″ of wire in the bottom basic loop. Leave the extended pieces of lacing wire on each section as they will be used to join the sections together. When all 9 sections are finished, join them closely together, side by side, by twisting the matching lacing wires together. Twist each one for at least 1″, then cut off the excess. Press the 1″ of twisted wires flat against the wrong side of the pumpkin sections. If you combine 3 sections at a time, then join the 3 units of 3 sections each, the assembly will be easier. Press the sections outward from the wrong side to form a ball before joining the 1st section to the 9th one; gather together the bottom basic wires inside the pumpkin and twist them together, tightly. Tape them and cut off all but 2″. Leave the top basic wires on the outside of the top of the pumpkin. Join the matching lacing wires of sections 1 and 9 to close the pumpkin, twist the top basic wires together, cut away all but 2½″ and cover them with tape. Tape a 7½″ piece of 16-gauge wire and push it into the center of the top of the pumpkin, leaving only 2½″ of the heavy wire at the top. Tape these 2½″ of heavy wire to the 2½″ of the top basic wires. This heavy wire will allow you to achieve the indentations at the top and bottom. Push the top wires down until a hollow forms in the top center of the pumpkin. Grasp the exposed end of the heavy wire at the bottom of the pumpkin with a pliers and bend it sharply to anchor it. Bend the open end up into the hollow pumpkin and squeeze it closed with the pliers.

Padding the Top Stem

Cut 4 pieces of paper drinking straws 2½″ long and tape them around the top wires. Curve the stem slightly. Make a small unit with green beads using a basic of 3 beads and enough rows (round top, round bottom), to equal the diameter of the blunt end of the pumpkin stem. Six rows should be enough. Tape it flat, across the blunt end of the stem. Transfer approximately 3 strands of green beads to a spool of 32-gauge wire. Attach the open end to the top of the stem and wrap the stem with the beaded wire all the way to the bottom.

EASTER BUNNY

For a touch of whimsy, stand a bunny or two amid the Easter eggs, beaded or real.

Materials

6 strands of white opaque beads
1 strand of pink beads
26-gauge silver or gold spool wire

The bunny is made in white in 2 parts, a back and a front, then combined. Each side has a body, head and one ear, made all in one. An arm, a leg and an eye are added later.

Front Half

Starting with the body, create a basic with 7 beads and work 16 rows, round top and bottom. You will finish at the top basic wire. Allow a long top basic wire, at least 12″, and use the same amount in the bottom basic loop. At the completion of the 16th row, wrap bare spool wire around the top basic wire for ⅓″.

To work the head, form a narrow, horizontal 7-bead loop on the left side of the top basic wire and secure it by wrapping bare spool wire once around the top basic wire. *Fig. 94.* Form a second narrow, horizontal 7-bead loop on the right side of the top basic wire and secure the 2nd loop by wrapping bare spool wire once around bottom basic wire. Wrap beaded wire around the 2 horizontal loops until there are 10 rows of beads, securing each row of beads, top and bottom, as you would for any normal petal, keeping the unit round at both top and bottom. *Fig. 95.* At the completion of the 10th row, bring the spool wire up the back of the unit just made (the head) and wrap bare spool wire up the top basic wire for ⅓″. Transfer 8 beads to the top basic wire. Work around the 8 beads to make a petal with 7 rows, pointed top, round bottom. *Fig. 96.* At the completion of the 7th row, wrap bare spool wire twice, to secure, then cut away excess wire. To the top basic wire transfer approximately 3″ of pink beads. Close to the top of the ear make a narrow loop with 1½″ of beads. Wrap beaded wire once around the outer edge of the narrow loop and secure by wrapping bare wire around the base of the double loop of beads. Cut away excess wire close to the beads and press the double loop of pink beads down the wrong side of the pointed ear.

Arm

Cut a piece of 26-gauge wire 15″ long. With the right side of your work facing up, evenly divide the 15″ of wire and insert 1 end, from

144

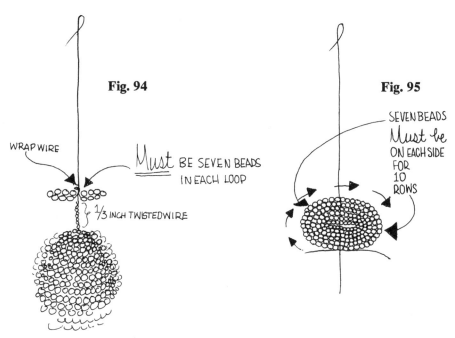

Fig. 94

Fig. 95

WRAP WIRE

Must BE SEVEN BEADS
IN EACH LOOP

⅓ INCH TWISTED WIRE

SEVEN BEADS
Must be
ON EACH SIDE
FOR
10
ROWS

front to back, on the left side of the top basic bead of the body. Insert the other end, from front to back, to the right of the top basic bead of the body. Pull the 2 wires all the way through to the back so that the center of the wire straddles the basic wire. Cross the wires to lock them in position. Lace the outside 4 rows of beads on each side, lacing at a slight upward slant. When the last row on the right side has been laced, feed on approximately 3½″ of white beads. Using 1½″ of beads, make a narrow loop of beads, and give this loop a 4 row crossover by beading up the front and down the back of the narrow beaded loop. Secure the crossover by wrapping bare wire twice, tightly, around the base of the "arm". Leave the remaining wire on, as it will later be used to join the front half to the back half of the bunny. The wire on the left side of the body will be used for the same purpose, therefore do not cut it off.

Leg

Cut a piece of spool wire 18″ long and straddle it onto the basic wire at the bottom of the basic row of beads of the body. Lace the last 4 rows on each side at a slight downward angle. To the lacing wire on the right side, transfer approximately 6½″ of white beads, and make a narrow loop with 3″ of beads. Give this narrow loop of beads a 4-row crossover by beading up the front and down the back of the loop. Secure by wrapping bare wire twice, tightly, around the base of the crossover loop, and do not cut the wire off.

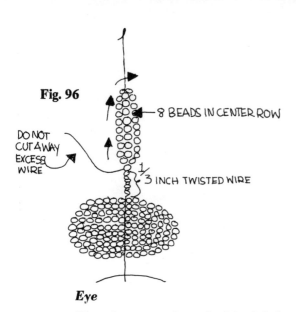

Fig. 96

8 BEADS IN CENTER ROW

DO NOT
CUT AWAY
EXCESS
WIRE

⅓ INCH TWISTED WIRE

Eye

Transfer approximately 21 pink beads to the spool of wire. Make a loop of 7 beads and encircle it with a row of beads. Twist both wires together to secure and insert the wires, from front to back, to the right of the basic wire and 4 rows down from the top of the bunny head. Bring the wire from the base of the ear to the eye wires and twist them together. Cut away all but ⅓″ of the twisted wires and flatten them against the wrong side of the head.

Back Half

Repeat the pattern for the front half. To shape each half before combining, round out the head and body sections by pressing thumbs into the centers of the wrong sides, cupping them slightly. Put the wrong sides together, twist the bottom wires together, and join the two halves by twisting together matching lacing wires at arms and legs for ½″. Cut away the excess wires, leaving only ¼″ on each. Tuck the end wires inside the body. Bend arms and legs forward. The bottom wires can be taped in white and curved into a circle to be used so that the bunny will stand alone, or taped in green and left uncurled to be used as a stem to insert into clay or styrofoam if the bunny is to be used in an arrangement.

EASTER EGGS

Make a bowl full for a centerpiece; use them as gifts or favors by filling them with miniature candies; or add a name card for place settings. These are wonderful for using leftover strands of beads, and they are as pretty in mixed colors as they are in solids.

Materials

4 or 5 strands of beads
12" to 20" of flat gold braid, ¼" width, or narrow metallic cord
1 plastic egg form (comes in two parts)
white glue
small paintbrush
toothpick
moistened cloth or sponge

Choose the beads you will be using, and knot both ends of the threads, using as little of the thread as possible for the knot.

Separate an egg form. Cut 2 pieces of gold cord or braid approximately 5½" long. With a small paintbrush, spread ¼" of glue on the edge of the top half of the egg form. Press 1 piece of cord gently, but firmly, into the glue and trim away any excess cord. With a toothpick or your fingers, remove any excess glue that has formed on the rim of the shell. Glue the other piece of cord to the rim of the bottom half of the egg form in the same way, and remove any excess glue. Do not put the 2 parts together for at least an hour after the 2 halves have been completely trimmed.

If you work your patterns by gluing first 1 row of beads to the top half of the form, then a row to the bottom half, you will give each row of beads or cord a chance to set, and you will not endanger the security of each previously glued row by touching it. Start each new row in the same place, directly above the previous row, using no more than ¼" of glue for each row, anchoring the start of each row by pressing about ½" of bare thread into the glue. Use the toothpicks to tamp down each row of beads so that the rows of beads are close together. As each row is glued into place, finish it by directing the bare thread at an upward angle. Anchor ¼" of the thread with a touch of glue, and set it aside. Add a row of beads to the other half of the shell form in the same way, and set it aside, returning to the 1st half. Cut the thread on the 1st half of the shell, close to the end bead, and start another row of beads directly above the 1st one. Knot off new strands of beads as needed. Complete each row of beads without having to patch, if possible. You can reserve the shorter amounts for the narrower tops and bottoms of the shells.

Pattern No. 1 has 1 row of cord, 2 rows of beads, 1 cord, 2 rows of beads, 1 cord, 2 rows of beads, and enough rows of beads to finish.

Pattern No. 2 is shaded. One was worked in 3 shades of green, another in 3 shades of blue. The blue one has 1 row of cord, 4 rows of light blue, 4 rows of medium blue, and enough dark blue to finish. The same sequence is followed for the other half of the shell. On the green egg, the colors have been reversed by starting with the darker green, then the medium, then the light.

Pattern No. 3 has metallic cord for the first row only, and the remainder of the shell form is covered with all beads of 1 color.

The last 5 or 6 rows of beads may be spiraled at both ends if you find it easier, and the extra rows of cord need not be precut. They can be glued on and then cut to fit. Using some beads in a corresponding color, cover a small bottle cap (the screw on type), and glue it on for a permanent pedestal for an egg. Keep your fingertips and toothpick clean and free of glue as you work.

CHRISTMAS BALLS

The small balls shown clustered in front of the Christmas candles in *Plate No. IX* are old glass ornaments whose original painted designs

had worn away through the years. They have been given a new look by gluing on strands of beads. Some are a solid color, others have 2 or 3 rows of gold or silver bugle beads around the center. They have been worked the same as the Easter Eggs, using the beads on their original threads. Each one used 3 or 4 strands of color and a strand or two of bugle beads. The larger balls are of styrofoam, 2½″ in diameter, made in one color, and each one takes 8 strands of beads.

CHRISTMAS CANDLES

Materials for Candles

> 3½ bunches of beads for 11″ candle
> 2½ bunches of beads for 8½″ candle
> 2 bunches of beads for 6½″ candle
> 32-gauge spool wire
> cardboard tubing
> red and green floral tape

Materials for Flames

> A few strands each of red, orange and yellow beads
> 26-gauge gold or silver spool wire

There are 5 beaded candles in *Color Plate No. IX*. The center one is 11″ high, the 2 on either side are 8½″ high and the smaller ones are 6½″. All are made with cardboard tubing for a foundation. The tubing from paper towels measures 1½″ in diameter. In preparation, the tubes have been covered with floral tape in green or red. The beads have been strung on 32-gauge spool wire. As a guide, plan about 1 bunch of beads for every 3″ of wrapping. Make 2 flames for each candle. Work in the following sequence:

Flame

Basic: 6 beads, pointed tops, round bottoms, 13 rows.
Transfer about 4″ of red beads onto a spool of 26-gauge wire. Work the basic row and rows 2, 3, 4 and 5 in the red. Allow 20″ of bare spool wire and cut the wire from the spool. Transfer enough orange beads onto the extended 20″ piece of wire to work rows 6, 7, 8 and 9, then feed on enough yellow beads to work rows 10, 11, 12 and 13. Leave the top basic wire and cut open the basic loop at the bottom, leaving 3 wires at the base of the flame. Make another flame in the

same way and stack 2 of them, one on top of the other, tops even, right sides in. Twist the 2 top basic wires tightly together for ½" Cut away the untwisted wires and bend the ½" of twisted wires down the wrong side of 1 petal. Reverse the petals so that the wrong sides face each other, and twist the bottom wires together to form a stem.

Top Cap

Make 1 for each candle in the color of the candle.
Basic: 3 beads, round top, round bottom, 22 rows.
Work with at least a 5" top basic wire and 10" of wire in the basic loop. The even number of rows will finish the cap at the top basic wire. At the completion of the 22nd row, allow 3" of bare spool wire and cut the wire from the spool. Cut open the basic loop at the bottom. Starting in the middle of the cap, lace across the center with 32-gauge spool wire and leave 2" of lacing wire on each side.

Assembly of Flame and Cap

Insert the stem wires of the flame into the center of the right side of the cap, pushing them all the way through until the bottom of the flame rests firmly on the cap. Bring 1 of the 2 bottom wires of the cap across the wrong side of the cap to meet the stem wires of the flame and twist them together. From the opposite side of the cap, bring another 1 of the 2 wires across the wrong side of the cap and twist it to the stem wires of the flame. Tape the 4 remaining wires of the cap. Cut a cardboard tubing to the desired length and cover it with tape. Set the flame and cap onto 1 open end of the taped tube. Bring the 4 wires of the cap down the sides of the taped tube and tape them securely to the tube.

150

Candle

Transfer 6 or 7 strands of beads to a spool of 32-gauge wire and attach its open end to any one of the wires of the cap, close to the beads of the cap, wrapping the wire 2 or 3 times around to secure. Press the open end of the spool wire down flat against the side of the tube and tape it to secure. Starting at the very top edge of the tube, wrap the beaded spool wire around and around the tubing, keeping the rows of beads and the beads themselves close together. It takes more than 1 bunch of beads to cover the tallest candle and it is rather awkward working with more than 6 or 7 strands of beads at a time. However, it is possible to start new beaded wire at the end of the previously added rows. When the first 6 or 7 rows have been wrapped, leave an inch or two of bare wire and cut the wire from the spool. Hold this end wire in place with a bit of tape, transfer another 6 or 7 strands to the spool wire, join the open end of the spool wire to the wire of the previously wrapped beads by twisting it close to the last bead on the candle. Point the twisted wires downward and tape them to the tube. Push the newly strung beads close to the last bead of the wrapped beads and continue wrapping the beaded wire around the tube. Repeat this procedure as often as necessary. When all but the last ⅓″ of the tube has been wrapped, cover this ⅓″ with Elmer's glue and attach the last few remaining rows of beads. Allow an inch or two of bare wire; tuck it inside the bottom of the tube and cover it with a bit of floral tape to secure.

BLACK-EYED SUSANS

The black-eyed susan is indigenous to the South and West regions of the United States where whole fields of them can be seen growing wild. Replicas like these will add a bright spot to any bouquet.

Materials
(for 1 flower)

>   *4 strands of yellow transparent or opaque beads*
>   *1 strand of black or brown beads*
>   *1 strand of green transparent beads*
>   *26-gauge spool wire*
>   *32-gauge spool wire*
>   *16-gauge stem wire*

Flower Petals

Basic: 1″, pointed tops, round bottoms, 5 rows.

Make 10 for each flower in yellow. Reduce the bottom wires to 2 on all petals.

Center

Basic: 3 beads, round tops, round bottoms, 10 rows.

Make this center mounded, like a beehive. *Fig. 76.* Make 1 for each flower in either black or dark brown. Cut open the basic loop at the bottom of the loop. Because this unit has an even number of rows, you will finish at the top basic wire, therefore there will be 2 wires at both ends of the beehive. Bring both sets of wires to the center of the wrong side of the beehive, and twist them together to form a stem.

Small Green Leaves

Four inches from the open end of the spool wire, make a 4-row crossover loop, measuring 2″ of beads for the initial loop. Twist bottom wires together and cover with half-width tape. Make at least 2 for each flower.

Large Green Leaves

Four inches from the open end of the spool wire, make a 4-row crossover loop, measuring 5″ of beads for the initial loop. Twist bottom wires together and cover with half-width tape.

Assembly of Leaves

With the bottom of the leaves even, tape 2 small and 1 large leaf together with half-width tape, setting the large leaf in between the 2 smaller ones.

Assembly of Flower

Tape the wires of the center unit and tape them directly to the top of a piece of taped 16-gauge wire. Cut a 15″ piece of 32-gauge wire and wrap 1 end around the base of the center, 3 or 4 times to secure. Attach the petals, one at a time, right sides up, around the base of the beehive center. Wrap twice around with the wire for each petal. When the last one has been added, wrap an extra time or two and cut off excess wire. Thin out the petal wires and cover the exposed wires with tape. Tape down the stem for 2″ and tape on a group of leaves, then continue taping to the bottom of the stem. If more than 1 group of leaves is to be added, space them 1⅓″ apart down the stem.

COLUMBINES

The garden variety is usually blue and white but the hybrids of this graceful flower offer many unusual color combinations. They are lovely in two shades of pink, lavender or yellow, or in solid white or yellow and white. *Color Plate No. VI* shows them in blue and white.

Materials
(for 1 cluster of 2 flowers, 1 bud)

6 strands of blue transparent beads
5 strands of white opaque beads
½ strand of yellow beads
26-gauge spool wire, gold or silver
4 stem wires, 16-gauge

Flower, White Petals

Unit 1

Basic: 8 beads, round tops, round bottoms, 7 rows.

Transfer 2 or 3 strands of white beads to the spool of wire and make 2 petals all in one, without cutting the wire, by using the single split basic technique. Create a basic of 8 beads, slide 8 beads into a generous basic loop (10″). Make the 1st petal around the original 8 bead basic, push the 8 beads in the basic loop to 1 side of the basic loop, cut open the loop at the bottom of the loop and work the second 7-row petal around the second 8 beads. You will finish with 2 wires. *Fig. 97.* Make the remaining 3 petals all in one without cutting the wires, by using the double split basic technique. Create a basic of 8 beads and slide 16 beads into a generous basic loop. Make a 7-row petal around the original 8-bead basic, slide 8 beads to each side of the basic loop, *Fig. 98.* Close to the base of the 1st petal, cut open the basic loop at the bottom of the loop, crimp both ends of the cut wires to prevent the beads from slipping off, and make a 7-row petal on each of the 2 new basics. Fig. 99. You will finish with 1 wire. Make 2 of each.

Flower, Blue Petals

Unit 2

Basic: 6 beads, pointed tops, round bottoms, 9 rows.

Each petal is made individually, but beads are slipped into the basic loop so that the tendrils on each petal can be made as part of the petal. Create a basic with 6 beads and slide 2½″ of beads into a generous basic loop (10″). Make a 9-row petal on the original 6-bead basic, allow 3″ of bare wire and cut the wire from the spool. Turn the petal upside down, evenly divide the 2½″ of beads in the basic loop so that there are 1¼″ of beads on each side. *Fig. 100.* Push the beads close to the base of the petal and twist together the wires at the opposite end. Coil the twisted wires 2 or 3 times around the pointed end of an embroidery needle or corsage pin and cut away the excess close to the last coil. Push the coils close together. Make 5.

Stamens

Transfer 24 beads to a spool of 26-gauge gold wire. Slide 1 bead to within 3″ of the open end of the wire and twist both wires for 1″. Move 1 bead 1″ from the bottom of the twisted wires and twist both wires for 1″. Repeat until there are 6 beads on top of 1″ of twisted wire. *Fig. 101*. Allow 3″ of bare spool wire and cut the wire from the spool. Make 1 more unit in the same way, join both units by twisting their bottom wires together. Arrange the stamens in an upright cluster. Make 4 units all in yellow.

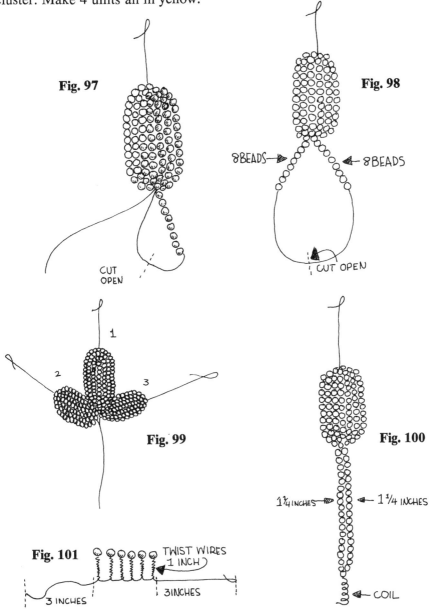

Fig. 97

Fig. 98

8 BEADS → ← 8 BEADS

CUT OPEN

CUT OPEN

1

2

3

Fig. 99

Fig. 100

1¼ INCHES → ← 1¼ INCHES

Fig. 101   TWIST WIRES
1 INCH

3 INCHES   3 INCHES

← COIL

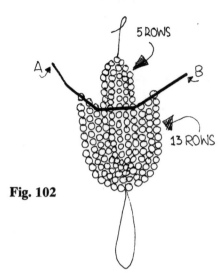

Fig. 102

Bud

Basic: 1 inch of beads, pointed top, round bottom, 3 rows. Make 5. Transfer a strand or two of green beads to the spool of wire and make a 3-row leaf with a 1″ basic. Reduce the bottom wires to 2 by cutting open the basic loop on one side close to the base of the leaf. Twist the bottom wires together for ¼″. Transfer 15 beads to the top basic wire and push them close to the green leaf. Coil the wire at the opposite end of the blue beads around an embroidery needle or corsage pin 3 times, keeping the coils close together. Trim off excess wire close to the last coil. Stack all 5 leaves, right sides up, bottoms even, and twist the bottom wires together all the way. Swing the leaves, wrong sides up, and in a circle. Gather the blue tendrils together and spiral the entire bud, separating the blue tendrils, slightly, at their coiled ends.

Small Leaves

Basic: 10 beads, pointed tops, round bottoms, 5 rows. Make 2 leaves in green for each flower and bud.

Large Leaves

Basic: 1″, pointed tops, round bottoms, 13 rows in all.
Before starting the leaf, cut a 10″ piece of spool wire and set it aside. Create a basic with 1″ of beads and work rows 2 and 3 with a pointed top and round bottom. Straddle the 10″ piece of precut wire in the center of the basic row of beads, pushing it from the front of the leaf to the back. Cross the wires once on the wrong side of the leaf. Keeping the 10″ of wire in a horizontal position, work the 4th row of beads to the cross wire on the left and wrap bare spool wire over the top and around it, then finish beading the top half of the 4th

row. Bead the top half of the 5th row, wrap bare spool wire around the cross wire on the right, then finish beading the bottom half of the 5th row. Adjust the cross wires to an upward angle as in *Fig. 102 (A)* and *(B)*. Make the 6th row by beading up to the cross wire on the left and wrap bare spool wire 1½ times around the cross wire. This will change the direction of your work. Bead down the left side of the leaf, thus creating the 7th row. Rows 6 and 7 have been made on the left side of the center section (the original 5 rows). Make rows 8 and 9 on the right side of the center unit by beading up to the cross wire, wrapping bare spool wire around it 1½ times, then beading down to the bottom basic wires again. Make rows 10 and 11 on the left side and rows 12 and 13 on the right. Remove all but ¼″ of the top basic wire on the center section and turn it down the wrong side of the leaf. Reduce the bottom basic loop to 2 by cutting open the loop close to the beads. Bring the cross wires down the wrong side of the leaf and twist all 4 wires together at the base of the leaf to form a stem. If you are designing an all-around arrangement, bead the cross wires before bringing them down the wrong side of the leaf. They will be less obvious if beaded. Make 2 leaves in green for each flower and bud.

Assembly of Flower

Stack the round white petals right sides up and bottoms even. Twist together the bottom wires to form a stem. Swing the petals into a circle, right side up, lift the petals up at the center and flute them out at the top. Slide the cluster of stamens between any 2 petals and tape the stamen and petal stems together with half-width tape.

Attach a 15″ piece of 32-gauge lacing wire to the base of the petals and wrap it 2 or 3 times tightly to secure. Add the blue petals, one at a time, right sides up and tendrils at a downward angle, around the base of the round petals and stamens. Wrap the lacing wire twice tightly with each addition, and an extra wrap or two on the 5th petal. Cut away excess 32-gauge wire and cover the stems of the flowers with half-width tape. If you are using gold wire for the entire flower, you may prefer the look of gold stems. If so, twist the flower stems tightly all the way to the end and tape only the last inch.

Assembly of Sprays

Bud: Allow 2″ of stem on the bud and tape it to the top of a 16-gauge stem wire that has been taped. Tape down the stem for 2″ and add a pair of small leaves directly opposite each other, right sides toward the stem, and no stem showing on the leaves. Tape down another 2″ and tape on 2 large leaves in the same way.

Flower: Mount 2 flowers on 2 individual, taped, 16-gauge wires in the same way, adding 2 small and 2 large leaves to each. Group the stems together and secure their stems with tape. For a spray of columbine, set the flowers farther apart, and for a cluster, have them closer together.

SNAPDRAGONS

Any pastel shade is excellent for these two-sided beauties. They are ideal for all-around arrangements because you don't have to duplicate them for the reverse side of the bouquet.

Materials
(for 1 stalk)

> 1 bunch of pale yellow beads for flowers
> 1 strand of deeper yellow for stamen
> 8 strands of green beads
> 26- or 28-gauge spool wire
> 14- or 16-gauge stem wire

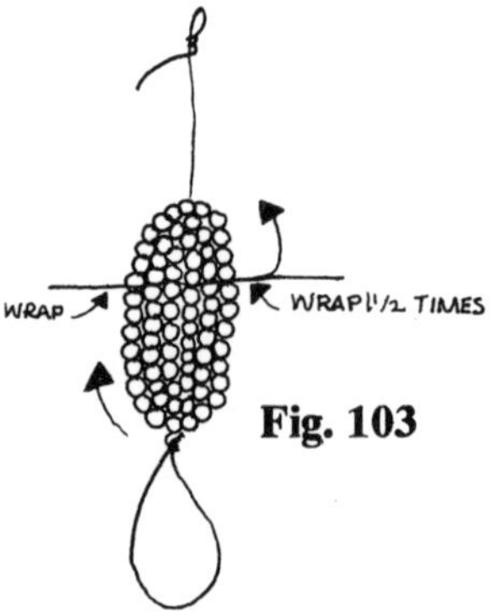

Fig. 103

Flower, Front Petal

Basic: 1¼″ round top, round bottom, 5 rows.

Cut an 8″ piece of spool wire and set it aside. Work the 5-row petal, and reverse wrap at the bottom of the petal. Without cutting the petal from the spool, attach the 8″ piece of precut wire to the petal by folding the wire in half, then straddling it over the basic row, 5 beads down from the top bead. Insert the wire from front to back, through the right side of the petal, and cross the wires once on the back of the petal, thus securing them to the basic wire between the 5th and 6th bead of the basic. Keep both ends of the wire horizontal, as in *Fig. 103.* Work a 6th row up the left side, wrapping bare spool wire around the cross wire as you come to it, crossing over the top of the cross wire. Bead to the top basic wire to complete the 6th row. Work the top half of the 7th row and wrap bare spool wire around the right side of the cross wire 1½ times, thus reversing the direction of your work. Bead to the top basic wire, and wrap around it as usual. Bead down the left side and wrap bare spool wire around the cross wire

1½ times. Bead up to the top basic wire and wrap spool wire as usual. Bead down the right side again, and wrap spool wire 1½ times around the cross wire, bead to the top basic wire, wrap wire as usual, and bead down to the cross wire on the left. Twist both the cross wire and spool wire together for ½". Allow 3" of bare spool wire and cut the wire from the spool. Your petal now has 6 rows on the bottom two-thirds, and 13 on the top third. Trim off the top basic wire as usual, and turn down the wrong side of the petal. Cut open the basic loop at the bottom of the loop. Make one for each flower, 10 in all.

Small Flower, Back Petal

Basic: 9 beads, round top, round bottom, 5 rows.
Create the basic with the 9 beads, and slip 8 beads into a generous basic loop. Work 2 rows of beads on each side of the original basic, giving it 5 rows in all. Turn the petal upside down, place 4 beads on each side of the basic loop and cut open the basic loop at *Fig. 104 (A).* This creates 2 new basic wires around which you will build 2 small round petals. Crimp both open ends of the basic wires to prevent the beads from slipping off. Wrap bare spool wire around the base of the left wire for ⅓" and build a 7-row petal with a round top and round bottom. *Fig. 105.* Wrap bare spool wire down the other basic wire for another ⅓" and build a second 7-row petal, round top and bottom. Finishing with the spool wire in front, allow 4" of bare wire and cut the wire from the spool. Onto the 4" of bare wire, feed 15 beads of a contrasting color. Pale green, deeper yellow or orange are effective. Make a narrow loop of the 15 beads close to the base of the 2 top petals. Wrap remaining wire around the base of one petal, twice, and cut away the excess, close to the beads. Make 1 small petal for each of the 5 top flowers.

Large Flower, Back Petal

Repeat the pattern for the small petals but give the 2 top petals 9 rows of beads instead of 7. Make 1 for each of the 5 bottom flowers on the stalk.

Calyx

Three inches from the open end of the spool wire, make 7 continuous narrow loops in green beads, using 12 beads for the 1st and 2nd loops, 15 beads for the 3rd loop, 18 beads for the 4th, 15 beads for the 5th, and 12 beads for the 6th and 7th loops. Allow 3″ of bare spool wire and cut the wire from the spool. *Fig. 106.* Join the 2 end wires and twist them together to form a circle just large enough to allow the stem of the flower to be inserted into the center of the circle. Make 1 for each flower and 10 for the stalk.

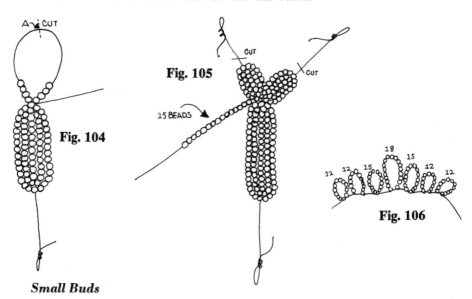

Fig. 105

Fig. 104

15 BEADS

Fig. 106

Small Buds

Using the directions for the calyx, make 3 in green. Twist the bottom wires together, tape them and crush the loops up to form a cluster.

Large Buds

Using the same directions for the calyx, make 3 in green and before closing the loops, insert one 15 bead loop of yellow beads in the center, twist both sets of wires together, bring all loops upward to form a tight cluster and tape the bottom wires. Make 3 for each stalk.

Small Green Leaves

Basic: 1¼″ pointed tops, round bottoms, 3 rows.
Using the single split basic technique, make 4 pairs for each stalk.

Large Green Leaves

Basic: 1½″, pointed tops, round bottoms, 5 rows.
Using the single split basic technique, make 4 pairs for each stalk.

Assembly of Leaves

Combine two pairs of small leaves by setting one pair on top of the other pair so that the bottoms are even. Twist both sets of wires together and tape with half-width tape. Combine a pair of large leaves in the same way, slide the stem of the small leaves between any 2 large leaves, leaving 1½″ of stem showing on the small leaves, and tape both stems together.

Assembly of Flowers

Front Petals: With the top portion of the petal as your guide, have the wrong side facing you; cup it deeply, spoon-shaped, with your thumb, and roll back the top edge, slightly. Bend it forward from the cross wire, and bring the cross wires to the back, but do not twist them together. Roll the lower section of the petal to the back, slightly, by holding a pencil against the back of this lower section and pressing the rows of beads against it. You will achieve the proper shape easily.

Back petals: With the right side of the petal facing you, cup the two top petals in, like a spoon, and turn the tips of the petals back, slightly. Shape the lower section of the petal by holding a pencil against the front of the petal and pressing the rows of beads forward against the pencil. When the front and back petals are combined, the lower sections will be tubular.

Combine 1 front and 1 back petal by setting 1 back petal behind a front one, bottoms even. Twist together the bottom wires to form a stem. Bring the cross wires of the front petal together behind the flower, twist them tightly, so that the 2 petals are close together. Twist the wires for ⅓″ and cut away all but ¼″ of the twisted wires, pressing them flat against the back of the flower. Insert the twisted wires of the flower into the center hole of one calyx. Push the calyx close to the base of the flower, pressing the green loops up and around the base. Cover the combined wires with tape.

Assembly of Stalk

Tape a 12″ piece of 16-gauge wire and tape 1 small bud to the top. Tape down the stem for ½″ and add 2 more small buds, spacing them ½″ apart. Add 2 or 3 of the buds with yellow centers in the same way. Add the 5 small flowers and the 5 larger ones to the stem, one at a time, ⅔″ apart with only ½″ of stem showing on each

individual flower. One inch below the last flower, and to the left, tape on 1 group of leaves. Tape another group on the right side of the stem, then continue taping to the bottom of the stem wire. Arrange the flowers so that they face outward around the master stem.

POPPIES

Color Plate No. VII shows 30 of these flowers, each with two leaves, for a beautiful arrangement which can be viewed from all sides. The stems have been wrapped with the small green beads. Ten have been beaded for 6½″, 10 for 7½″ and 10 for 8½″. The colors of the flowers have been divided almost equally in each length group. These flowers look well in almost any color combination, however, the bolder, the better.

Materials
(for 1 flower)

8 strands of beads for petals
3 strands of black beads for center units
6 strands of green beads for leaves and calyx
1 strand of yellow or orange beads for stamen spikes
26-gauge spool wire
32-gauge spool wire
16-gauge stem wire

4 ROWS OF BEADS

Flower, Center Mound

Fig. 107

Unit 1

Basic: 3 beads, round top, round bottom, 12 rows.
Create a basic with 3 beads, use 5 beads for row 2, 6 beads for row 3; 7 beads for row 4; 8 beads for row 5; 9 beads for row 6; 10 beads for row 7; 11 beads for row 8; 12 beads for rows 9, 10, 11 and 12. You will finish at the top basic wire, and there will be 2 wires at both ends. Allow 3″ of bare spool wire and cut the wire from the spool. Cut open the basic loop at the bottom of the loop. Make 1 for each flower in black.

Unit 2

These are made using the continuous wraparound method. Four inches from the open end of the spool wire, make an oval 12-bead loop in black. Wrap beaded wire around the oval loop 3 times, securing each row of beads by wrapping bare spool wire around the wire at the base of the loop. To the left of, and ⅓″ away from the first wraparound petal, make another 12 bead loop and wrap beaded wire around it 3 times, securing each wraparound as you work. Continue until you have 6 of the 4-loop wraparounds. *Fig. 107.* Allow 3″ of bare spool wire and cut the wire from the spool. Make 1 in black for each flower.

Unit 3 Stamen Spikes

There are 16 pair of spikes and the shading can be pre-strung. To make 1 pair, transfer to a spool of 26-gauge wire, 1 black, 3 yellow (or orange), 2 black and 2″ of yellow (or orange). Then 2 black, 3 yellow (or orange) and 1 black. Wrap the open end of the spool wire around the pointed end of a corsage pin or darning needle, 3 times, keeping the coils close together. Remove the pin. In the middle of the 2″ of yellow beads, make a basic loop. At the opposite end of the unit, coil the wire around the pin 3 times and cut the spool wire close to the coil. *Figs. 108* and *109.* This constitutes 1 pair. Make 15 more pair for each flower. Cut open the bottom of the loop of wire on each pair, and twist both wires together to the end.

Unit 4 Petals

Basic: 6 beads, round tops, pointed bottoms, 15 rows.
Reduce the bottom basic wires to 2, and trim off all but ¼″ of the

top basic wires, pressing them down the wrong side of the petal, as usual. Make 8 petals for each flower.

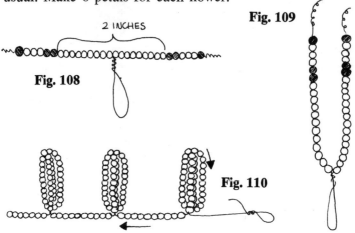

Fig. 109

2 INCHES

Fig. 108

Fig. 110

Calyx

Three inches from the open end of the spool wire, make 12 continuous loops in green, measuring 2″ of beads for each loop. Allow 3″ of bare spool wire, and cut the wire from the spool. Make 1 for each flower.

Leaves

The leaves are made with continuous 4-row crossover loops, all on one wire, in green. Three inches from the open end of the spool wire, make a narrow loop of 2½″ of beads, bring beaded wire up the center of the narrow loop of beads, cross over the top of the loop with bare spool wire, bring beaded wire down the back of the loop and secure the crossover row of beads by wrapping bare spool wire around the base of the beaded loop. Push 9 beads to the base of the beaded loop, and at the opposite end, make another 4-row crossover beaded loop. Repeat until you have 9 crossover loops, each one separated by 9 beads. Allow 3″ of bare spool wire and cut the wire from the spool. Fold the string of loops in half as in *Fig. 110,* and twist the bottom wires together to form a stem. At the base of the top loop, and between each pair of loops, give the double row of 9 beads 1 full twist to cross them. Curve the loops up and out to shape. Tape the bottom wires. Make 2 for each flower.

Assembly

Tape a 12″ piece of 16-gauge stem wire. Set one unit 1 in the center of one unit 2, twist both sets of wires together and tape them. Tape these 2 units to the top of the taped stem wire. Attach a 30″ piece of 32-gauge wire to the base of these units, and wrap it around 3 or 4 times to secure. Add the 16 pairs of unit 3 close to the base of the first 2 units, and around the stem wire, wrapping the 32-gauge wire twice tightly, with each addition. Add the 8 petals in the same way, right sides up, and around the base of the first 3 units. Wrap wire 2 or 3 times more to secure and cut away the excess. Thin out the wires of all units and cover them with tape to secure to the stem. Close the calyx loops by back-weaving the finish wire half-way around, thus balancing the wires and forming the loops into a circle. Insert the open end of the stem wire into the center of the calyx loops, and push the calyx loops close to the base of the flower. Let the calyx wires hang straight down and tape them to the flower stem. Wrap green beads around stems if you wish. If not, on ⅓ of the flowers, tape on 2 leaves to each, 6½″ down from the base of the flower. On another ⅓ of the flowers, add leaves 7½″ down from the base of the flowers and on the remaining third add them 8½″ down on the stem. Cup the petals up and arrange the 6 petals of unit 2 so that they are evenly spaced around the base of unit 1.

PAINTED DAHLIAS

This lovely flower uses 2 colors of beads to give it the "painted" look. Any 2 colors work well as long as they are compatible. In the studio it has been done in white with red, with black cattails added. It was most attractive in a black container.

Fig. 111

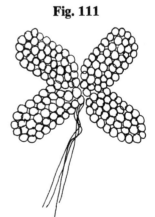

Materials

(for 1 flower)
¾ of a bunch of light orange beads
½ bunch of bittersweet (deep orange) beads
1 bunch of light green beads
26-gauge spool wire
16-gauge steel wire
32-gauge spool wire for assembling

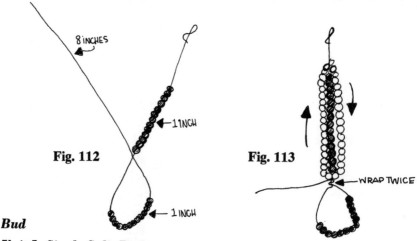

Fig. 112   **Fig. 113**

8 INCHES

1 INCH

1 INCH

WRAP TWICE

Bud

Unit 1, Single Split Basic

Basic: 5 beads, round top, round bottom, 7 rows.

By doing the bud first, we will be setting the pattern for the larger flowers. Transfer 2 or 3 strands of the darkest shade to the spool of 26-gauge wire. Push 5 beads to within 2″ of the open end of the wire and slip 5 more beads into the basic loop, using at least 5″ of bare wire for the basic loop. Create a 7-row petal around the original 5-bead basic, giving the petal a round top and round bottom. Push the 5 beads that are in the basic loop to one side of the loop and cut open this loop at the bottom. Wrap bare spool wire around the wire at the base of these 5 beads and build another 7-row petal, using the second 5 beads as the basic for the 2nd petal. Allow 3″ of bare spool wire and cut the wire from the spool. Trim off top basic wires as usual. Make 1 more pair of petals in the same way for each bud. Combine the 2 pair of petals by stacking them, one on top of the other, wrong sides up, bottoms even, and twist together the 4 wires at the bottom for ⅓″. Open them into a circle, *Fig. 111,* then cup each petal out and up to form a cluster, making sure the wrong sides of the petals are in.

Bud

Unit 2, Single Split Basic

Basic: 1″, pointed top, round bottom, 3 rows.

String more dark orange if needed, and create a basic with the 1″ of beads. Slide 1″ of beads into the basic loop, allow 8″ of bare spool wire and cut the wire from the spool. *Fig. 112.* String approximately 5″ of the light orange beads onto the 8″ of bare wire. Make a 3-row petal on the original basic beads. Cut open the basic loop at the bottom of the loop after having pushed the 1″ of beads to one side, and make another 3-row petal on the second basic. This makes 1 pair of petals. Make 4 more pair, 5 pair in all, for each bud. *Figs. 113 and 114.*

Assembly of Bud

Tape Unit 1 to the top of a taped stem wire. Attach a 15″ piece of 32-gauge wire to the base of Unit 1 by wrapping one end 2 or 3 times around the base of the unit. Add the 5 pair of Unit 2 one at a time, around the base of Unit 1, setting them close with wrong sides up. Curve the petals of Unit 2 over the top of the petals of Unit 1. Leave the 32-gauge wire attached as it will be used to add sepals later on.

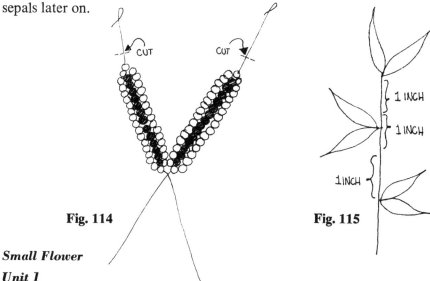

Fig. 114   Fig. 115

Small Flower

Unit 1

Repeat Unit 1 of the bud for the center of the small dahlia.

Unit 2

Repeat Unit 2 of the bud but increase the number of pairs from 5 to 8.

Unit 3

Repeat the technique of Unit 2, but increase the basic to 1½″, and make 8 pairs.

Assembly of Small Flower

Assemble Units 1 and Units 2 the same as for the buds, using a slightly longer piece of 32-gauge wire, and add the pairs of Unit 3 close around the base of the combined Units 1 and 2. Leave the 32-gauge wire attached. Set the petals on right sides up.

Large Flower

Repeat Units 1, 2 and 3 of the small flower but add 1 more unit, setting the petals on right sides up.

Unit 4

Increase the basic to 1¾″ and make 10 pairs.

Assembly of Large Flower

Assemble Units 1, 2, and 3, the same as for the small flower, and add the 10 Units 4 with the 32-gauge wire, setting the petals on right sides up. Leave the 32-gauge wire attached.

Remember to have the basic row of beads on all of the pointed petals worked in the darker color, and rows 2 and 3 in the lighter shade. Trim off all top basic wires, as usual, leaving only ¼″ to turn to the wrong sides of the petals.

Sepals

The green sepals are made exactly like Unit 2 of the flowers, but in solid green, no shading. Make 3 pair for each bud and 4 pair for each flower. Attach them to the underside of the flowers with the extended pieces of 32-gauge wire, adding them close to the base of the flowers, right sides up. Trim off and thin out the wires from the petals and stems on each flower, and cover them with tape.

Leaves

The green leaves are made just like the sepals and are combined in branches consisting of 3 pairs to each branch. Each flower has 2

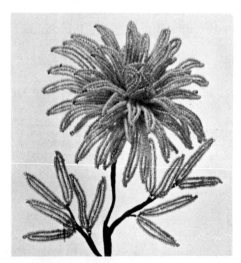

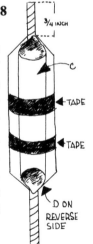

Fig. 117

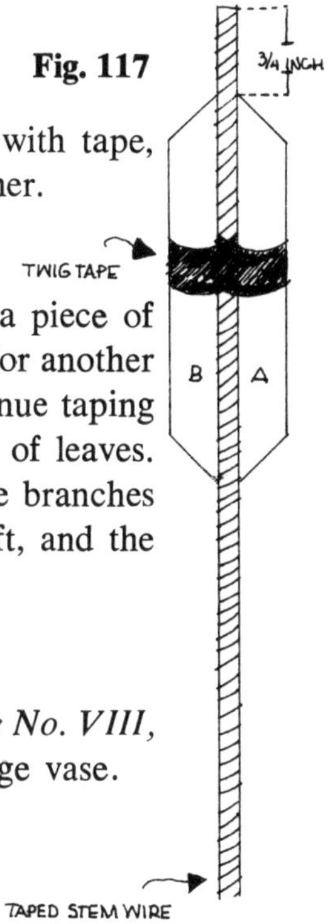

branches of 3 pairs each. Combine them as in *Fig. 115,* with tape, taping each pair individually, then taping the pairs together.

Adding Leaves to Flower Stems

TWIG TAPE

Two and a half inches below the head of a bud, attach a piece of tape, and tape on 1 branch of leaves. Tape down the stem for another 1½″, and tape on the second branch of leaves, then continue taping down the stem for another 1½″ and add the 3rd branch of leaves. Add leaves to the flower stems in the same way. Swing the branches of leaves to opposite sides, one to the right, one to the left, and the 3rd to the right.

CAT-O-NINE TAILS

Use these for their interesting lines, as shown in *Color Plate No. VIII,* or mount a dozen or two on very long stems to fill a large vase.

Materials

½ bunch of dark brown beads
twig tape
32-gauge spool wire
16-gauge stem wire if short, 14- or 12-gauge if very long
2 ordinary wax paper drinking straws

TAPED STEM WIRE

Fig. 118

Stems

Prepare the stem wire by covering it with twig tape. Cut the 2 straws in half. If they are 8″ straws, this will give you 4 pieces, each 4″ long. Working on a slant, cut off ¾″ on both ends of each of the 4″ pieces. *Fig. 116.* Using the twig tape, attach the 4 pieces of straw to the taped stem wire, one at a time, setting each straw ¾″ below the top of the stem wire and taking care not to crush the straws. Attach the first 2 straws back to back, and opposite one another. *Fig. 117, (A and B).* Attach the remaining 2 straws, back to back, in between the first 2. *Fig. 118, (C) and (D).* Cover all 4 straws with the twig tape, crushing the slanted ends so that they taper down the heavy stem wire.

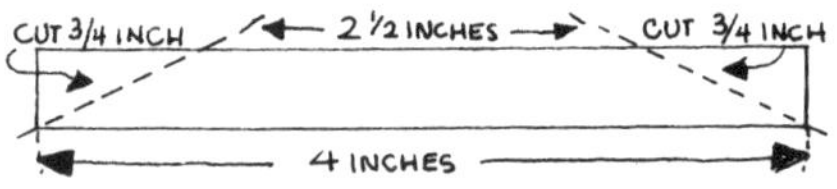

Fig. 116

CUT ¾ INCH — 2 ½ INCHES — CUT ¾ INCH
4 INCHES

Cattails

Transfer 5 or 6 strands of brown beads to the spool of 32-gauge wire, leaving 3 or 4″ of bare wire at the open end of the beaded

wire. Starting ¾″ below the top of the stem wire, at the top of the straws, wrap the bare open end of the beaded spool wire around the stem wire 3 or 4 times tightly. Push the strung beads to the stem wire and wrap beaded wire around and around the tapered straw section of the stem wire. Keep the rows of beads and the beads on the spool wire close together with an easy tension. You will find that after you have completed the first 2 or 3″ of wrapping in an upright position, it will be easier to keep the rows of wrapped beads closer together if you reverse the position, and turn the cattail upside down, then finish the remainder of the padded section. When the bottom of the tapered end has been reached, push any remaining beads on the spool wire toward the spool, and finish off by wrapping bare spool wire, tightly, 3 or 4 times around the heavy stem wire, then cut the wire from the spool. Cover any exposed 32-gauge wire with tape.

GIANT CONE FLOWERS

The cone flower grows in a variety of colors, pink, lavender and red as well as orange. All, however, have the large, pale green cone that makes it so unique.

Materials
(for one flower)

> *7 strands of light orange beads*
> *2 strands very pale green beads*
> *½ strand of yellow*
> *6 strands light or medium green*
> *26-gauge spool wire*
> *1 stem wire, 16-gauge*

Cone

Basic: 2 beads, round top, round bottom, 36 rows.
Transfer a strand or two of very light green beads to a spool of 26-gauge wire and create a basic of 3 beads. Use the following number

of beads for each row until you have completed 15 rows. Row 2, 5 beads; row 3, 6 beads; row 4, 7 beads; row 5, 8 beads; row 6, 9 beads; row 7, 10 beads; row 8, 11 beads; row 9, 12 beads; row 10, 13 beads; row 11, 14 beads; row 12, 15 beads; row 13, 16 beads; row 14, 17 beads; and row 15, 18 beads. Rows 16 through 38 will use 19 beads on each row. At the completion of the 15th row, allow 30 inches of bare wire and cut the wire from the spool. Feed approximately 6″ of yellow beads onto the extended piece of wire. Work the next 6 rows in the yellow beads, using 19 beads for each row. At the completion of the 21st row, remove any excess yellow beads, transfer approximately 14″ of the light green beads to the extended piece of wire and finish the remaining rows, using 19 beads for each row. There are an even number of rows in the pattern, therefore you will finish at the single basic wire. Cut open the basic loop at the bottom of the loop and combine all 4 wires in the center of the bottom opening of the cone by twisting them together for 2″.

Large Flower Petals

Basic: 15 beads, pointed tops, round bottoms, 9 rows.
Reduce the bottom wires to 2 by cutting open the side of the basic loop close to the base of the petal, and twist the 2 wires together for ½″. Trim off the top basic wire to ¼″ and turn the ¼″ of wire down the wrong side of the petal as usual. Make 6 in light orange.

Small Flower Petals

Basic: 20 beads, pointed top, round bottom, 5 rows.
Transfer 2 or 3 strands of light orange beads and make a basic with the 20 beads. Work rows 2 and 3. Allow 8″ of bare wire and cut the wire from the spool. Onto the extended 8″ of bare wire, transfer 15 of the light green beads for the bottom half of row 4, enough light orange beads to work the top half of the 4th and 5th rows, then enough of the pale green to finish the bottom half of the 5th row. Reduce the bottom wires to 2 and cut away all but ¼″ of the top basic wire, turning it back as usual. Make 6.

Leaves

Basic: 9 beads, pointed tops, round bottoms, 7 rows.
Reduce the bottom wires to 2 by cutting open the basic loop on one side close to the base of the leaf. Trim off all but ¼″ of the top basic wire and turn back as usual. Cover the bottom wires with half-width

tape to keep them thin, and make 3 groups of 3 leaves each, setting the middle leaf in each group ¾" higher than the other 2. Make 9 for each flower in either light or medium green.

Sepals

Basic: 9 beads, pointed top, round bottom, 7 rows.
Reduce the bottom basic wires to 2, the same as for the petals. Make 4 in same shades of green as leaves.

Assembly

Tape a 16-gauge stem wire and the bottom wires of the cone. Tape the cone to the top of the stem wire. Attach a 20" piece of 32-gauge lacing wire to the stem wire at the base of the cone, wrapping 2 or 3 times around to secure. Add the 6 small petals, right sides up, evenly spaced around the base of the cone, wrapping the 32-gauge wire twice with each addition. Between each small petal add a large petal, right sides up, around and close to the base of the cone. Add 4 sepals, right sides up, directly under the petals. Cut away excess 32-gauge wire, thin out the petal and sepal wires and cover all wires with tape. To the left and 3" below the base of the flower, tape on a group of 3 leaves. Tape down the stem for 1½" and tape on a second group of 3 leaves on the right side. Tape down another 1½" and add the 3rd set of 3 leaves to the left. Continue taping to the bottom of the stem. Arch the flower petals and sepals up and out to shape them, then bend the flower head forward, slightly.

BEADED LAMPSHADE

Materials

> 26- or 27-gauge gold spool wire
> 11 bunches cut crystal beads
> 1 bunch aqua transparent beads
> 3 strands coral pearl beads
> 1 frame
> 140 aqua teardrops
> white floral tape
> 3 yards white binding tape or ribbon, ½" width
> sewing thread
> beading needle

Of course there are many color combinations to choose from and a wide choice of shapes and sizes available in many shades. This

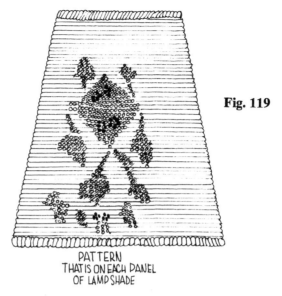

Fig. 119

PATTERN
THAT IS ON EACH PANEL
OF LAMP SHADE

one is 6-sided, each panel measuring 6¾″ high, 4½″ wide across the bottom and 3″ wide across the top. The overall measurements are 6¾″ high, 5″ in diameter across the top and 7½″ in diameter across the bottom. If you choose a larger or smaller frame, the required materials will have to be adjusted.

Preparing the Frame

Cover all ribs and the top rim of the frame with white floral tape. If you choose a colored bead instead of the white crystal, use a floral tape and binding tape in a color that corresponds with the beads. Wrap the bottom of the frame with binding tape or ribbon and sew it with needle and thread to secure the end. It is preferable to use the binding tape on the bottom of the frame as the fringe is made with needle and thread and sewn on to the frame. It is more difficult to sew through floral tape.

It is impossible to pre-string the required amount of beads, therefore work down the frame an inch or so at a time, stopping at a rib when the strung beads have been used up, then stringing more beads and starting again at the spot on the rib where you left off. Of course, the contrasting colors must be fed onto the open end of the wire. Transfer 4 or 5 strands of beads to the spool of wire, allow 2½ or 3 yards of bare wire. Cut the wire from the spool and crimp both ends. Loosely wrap the wire around your hand or a small piece of cardboard. This will allow you to have better control over the beaded wire as you wrap it around and around the top of the frame. Attach one end of the wire to the top of any one rib several times to secure.

173

Cover the wrapped wire with a small piece of tape. Wrap the beaded wire around the top rim of the frame until it is completely covered, keeping the rows of beads and the beads themselves close together. When you have worked around to the starting point, wrap bare wire around the same rib, to secure. Add more beads to your 3 yards of wire as you work, if they are needed, by feeding them onto the opposite end. If there are any remaining beads on the wire start working around the frame by beading between each rib, using just enough beads to fill the space between each rib. Wrap bare wire around each rib as you come to it. String more beads as needed, stopping and starting each time at a rib.

Work 14 rows around in crystal, wrap bare wire around the rib and cut the wire off. From here on, color will be added as needed, and you will string only the amount of beads needed to create the design in each panel of the frame.

Starting with the 15th row, attach a 36″ piece of bare wire to the rib on which you ended. Onto the open end of the wire transfer 17 crystal beads, 1 green bead and enough crystal beads to finish the row to the next rib. Wrap bare wire around the next rib; string 17 crystal beads, I green bead and enough crystal beads to work to the next rib. Continue all the way around. For the 16th row, decrease the amount of crystal beads by 1, and increase the green beads by 1, and work all the way around. This will start the leaf pattern. Actual counting of beads is rather impractical. You will have a neater pattern if you string the beads as you need them. The sketch, *Fig. 119.* is not meant to be an actual count of beads. Its purpose is to show you how to increase and decrease colors by row. Use it as a guide for the overall pattern. The open circles are green for leaves and their stems and the solid circles are aqua for the flowers. Follow the pattern to completion and finish with whatever number of rows of clear crystal are needed.

The little coral buds can be worked into the pattern, here and there, wherever you would like them, but it is easier to make them separately and twist them on later. The buds are 2 continuous 7 bead loops.

Rib Trim

Cut 6 pieces of wire 24″ long. Transfer enough crystal beads onto each wire to make a narrow twisted loop the length of one rib. It

174

will take approximately 12″ of beads for each loop. Attach the wire end to the top of the frame, and, using a 3″ piece of wire, secure the bottom end of the loop to the bottom of the frame. Top dress all 6 ribs in the same way.

Bottom Fringe

Thread a beading needle with white sewing thread and attach the thread to the bottom edge of the frame at a rib point. Thread 12 crystal beads, 1 aqua teardrop and 12 crystal beads, and sew to the bottom of the frame ¼″ to the right of the start of the thread. Repeat, with 12 crystal, 1 aqua teardrop, 12 crystal, and sew to the bottom of the frame ¼″ to the right. Continue all the way around the frame. This count will give you a 1-inch fringe. For a longer fringe, increase the number of crystal beads accordingly. May I suggest that you experiment until you find the length that is most pleasing to your eye. However, make sure you keep the fringe length in proportion to the size of the frame itself and the lamp base with which it is to be used.

Top Flowers

There are 12 clusters of teardrop flowers trimming the top of the frame. Each cluster has 3 teardrops and each teardrop is encircled with a row of crystal beads. Transfer 1 teardrop onto an 8″ piece of wire. Push it to within 2″ of one end of the wire, twist both wires together twice tightly at the base of the teardrop. Transfer enough crystal beads onto the opposite end of the wire to wrap around the outer rim of the teardrop. Wrap bare wire around the bottom wire to secure the row of crystal beads. Add a second teardrop, crossing the bottom wires to secure, and feed on enough crystal beads to wrap around the outer rim of the second teardrop. Make a third in the same way, keeping all teardrops close together at the bottom, then twist the 2 bottom wires together for an inch or so. Make 12 clusters in all, and using the end wires on each, attach each cluster to the top rim of the frame at rib point and in between. Hide the wires of the clusters between the rows of beads and cut away any excess wires.

HANGING BEADED LAMPSHADE

Materials

> 2 bunches of light pink transparent beads
> 2 bunches of medium pink transparent beads
> 24-gauge spool wire for top frame, silver or gold
> 26-gauge spool wire, silver or gold

Top Frame
(make 1)

Cut 8 pieces of 24-gauge wire 6½ʺ long; stack them so that they are even at the bottom and twist all wires at one end tightly, for 1ʺ. With the 1ʺ of twisted wires pointing downward, spread the untwisted wires so that they resemble the spokes of a wheel. *Fig. 120.* To a spool of 26-gauge wire transfer at least 8 strands of light pink beads. Attach the open end of the beaded spool wire around the top of the twisted wires of the frame several times to secure. Working from left to right around the frame, choose any one rib and wrap bare spool wire around it once, close to the center of the spokes. Put a small bend at the outer end of this spoke to mark the starting point of your work. Place 4 beads between this spoke and the one next to it, crossing the spool wire over the top, under and over. Place 4 beads between the 2nd and 3rd spokes and wrap bare spool wire around the 3rd spoke. *Fig. 121.* Continue placing 4 beads between each spoke until the 1st row has been completed. For the 2nd row place 5 beads between each spoke. For the 3rd row place 6 beads between each spoke. For the remaining rows (and there are 36 in all), it will not be necessary to count the beads for each spoke. Merely use enough beads between each spoke to fill the spaces between each wire, and be sure to cross the bare spool wire over the top and around the spoke as you secure each section of beads. Keep the frame flat until 22 rows have been worked. At the completion of the 22nd row, bend each spoke down so that it is perpendicular to the twisted wires in the center of the frame, and continue adding beads between each spoke until there are 14 more rows. These 14 will form the dropped sides of the frame. When you run short of beads, allow 3 or 4 yards of bare wire, cut the wire from the spool and feed beads onto the open end, a strand or two at a time. At the completion of the last row, bring spool wire across the center of the wrong side of the frame, wrap it several times around the twisted wires of the frame and cut away the excess. Do not cut away the spoke wires as these will be used to attach the petals to the frame.

Petals

Cut 2 pieces of 26-gauge spool wire 8ʺ long. Set them side by side and twist them together for the full length. These 2 wires will be used for the center basic wire to give it more strength. Transfer 7 strands of medium pink beads to the spool of 26-gauge wire. Three inches from one end of the double twisted wire, twist on the open end of the spool wire. Form a narrow, horizontal beaded loop to the left of the center wire using 30 beads for the loop. Follow the arrows in *Fig. 122* for the direction of the beaded wire and secure the loop by wrapping bare spool wire once around the center wire. Directly opposite this first loop form another narrow, horizontal 30-bead loop, following the arrows in *Fig. 122* for the direction of the beaded wire, and secure the second 30-bead loop by wrapping bare spool wire around the center wire. These two 30-bead loops have created a horizontal basic around which the remaining rows of beads will be built. Wrap beaded wire around and around, securing each row by wrapping bare spool wire around the center wire at top and bottom at the completion of each row until there are 36 rows of beads in all. Keep both the top and the bottom round. These are large petals and will need to be laced in several places. You will find that working the center lacing as you built the petal will keep the petal firmer and the end result will be neater. Work 3 or 4 rows on each side of the petal, cut a 12″ piece of 26-gauge spool wire, fold it in half and insert both open ends into the center of the right side of the petal so that the wire straddles the basic row of beads. Cross the wires once on the wrong side of the petal to secure, and with the right side of the petal facing you, lace together the rows of beads on each side, working first one side, then the other. Add 2 more rows of beads to each side of the petal, then lace them. Continue adding rows of beads, 2 at a time, then lacing them, until the petal is completed. *Fig. 123.* shows a 2nd and a 3rd lacing. These 2 should be done when the petal is completed. Start each lacing wire in the center and lace to the outside edge. Be sure to lace every row. Secure the ends of the lacing wires at points (*A*) and (*B*), *Fig. 123* and trim away the excess wires. Leave all other wire as they will be used in assembling the shade. Make 3 more petals in the same way.

Assembly

Working first with the top frame, choose any one spoke and feed on 20 light pink beads. Push them close to the bottom edge of the frame and bring the 20 beads up the outside of the frame so that they cover the outside of the spoke. Insert the open end of the wire through to the wrong side of the frame between the 13th and 14th rows,

178

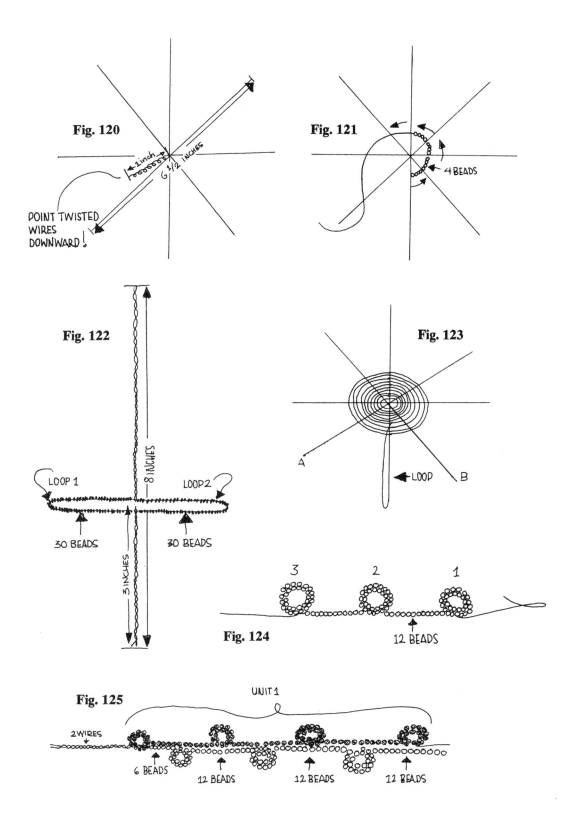

Fig. 120

1 inch

6 1/2 INCHES

POINT TWISTED
WIRES
DOWNWARD!

Fig. 121

4 BEADS

Fig. 122

8 INCHES

LOOP 1

LOOP 2

30 BEADS

30 BEADS

3 INCHES

Fig. 123

A

LOOP

B

Fig. 124

3   2   1

12 BEADS

Fig. 125

UNIT 1

2 WIRES

6 BEADS

12 BEADS

12 BEADS

12 BEADS

counting up from the bottom of the frame. Set 1 petal under the dropped side of the frame so that the top 8 rows of the petal are under the frame. Join the top basic wires of the petal to the spoke wire that is on the inside of the frame and twist them together tightly for 1″. Cut away all but ½″ of the twisted wires and press them down the wrong side of the petal, firmly. Attach the top left lacing wire of the petal to the first spoke wire to the left of the petal by twisting tightly for 1″. Cut away all but ½″ and tuck these wires into the wrong side of the frame. Attach the top right lacing wire to the first spoke wire to the right of the petal, twist together, cut away all but ½″ and tuck to the back of the frame.

To the next available spoke wire, feed on 20 light pink beads. Push beads close to the edge of the frame, bring wire up the outside of the frame, insert wire between 13th and 14th rows of the frame and set another petal under the frame, attaching it the same as the first petal. Allow the left side of the 2nd petal to overlap the right side of the first petal by ¾″, and use the lacing wires of both to join them together, twisting the lacing wires together on the wrong side and cutting away excess wires. Add the next 2 petals in the same way, using both top and center lacing wires to join and secure.

Top Trim

Unit 1

Transfer 2 strands of medium pink beads to spool wire and 4″ from the open end of the wire make an 8-bead loop, twisting the wires 1½ times, close to the base of the beaded loop. Encircle the 8-bead loop with a row of beads and secure the wraparound by wrapping bare spool wire around the base of the double loop. Push 12 beads to the base of the double loop, make an 8-bead loop at the opposite end of the 12 beads and encircle the 8-bead loop with a row of beads. *Fig. 124.* Continue in this manner until you have a piece long enough to encircle the bottom portion of the frame (about 20 loops). Allow 4″ of bare wire and cut the wire from the spool.

Unit 2

Transfer 2 strands of light pink beads to the spool of wire, leave 4″ of bare wire and attach it to the bare wire at the beginning of Unit 1 by twisting both wires together. *Fig. 125,* close to the base of the first double loop of Unit 1. Push 6 beads to the base of the twisted wires, make an 8-bead loop and encircle it with a row of beads,

180

securing the wraparound by wrapping bare spool wire around the base of the double loop. Cross bare spool wire between the 6th and 7th beads of Unit 1, wrapping the wire once. Make an 8-bead loop and encircle it with a row of beads. *Fig. 125.* Push 12 beads to the base of this double loop, wrap bare spool wire between the 6th and 7th beads of Unit 1. Make an 8-bead loop, encircle it with a row of beads, secure the wraparound, and push 12 more beads to the base of the double loop. Continue in the same way to the end of Unit 1. Your double loops will alternate; in between each dark pink loop there will be 1 light pink one. Keep all dark pink loops and beads on one side and all light pink ones on the opposite side. *Fig. 125.* Twist end wires together to form a circle of the top trim. Attach to shade with small pieces of lacing wire to secure, shape the large petals by cupping them out in the center and in at the bottom edges. Bend the inner twisted wires of the frame to one side and press them flat against the top of the frame. Attach an electrical socket to the desired length of electrical cord. Bring opposite end of cord through the opening at the top of the frame and attach a plug to the end.

THE HORN OF PLENTY

If you are a "paste pot" enthusiast, as I am, you will particularly enjoy making the vegetables shown in *Color Plate No. XI.* Except for the artichokes, peas and lima beans, all of the beads are glued onto forms that are easy to find in hobby shops. If you are a hobbyist, you probably already have some of the shapes. Others are simple to make from objects found around the house. The heavy cardboard rod that is on wire clothes hangers is ideal for mushroom stems. Start saving champagne corks. They're fine too. Cork balls, styrofoam forms and candles can all be useful.

Wax candles come in a wide variety of sizes and shapes. For creating the carrots, use the tapered kind as is, but trim fatter shapes with an X-acto tool or small paring knife. Elmer's Glue adheres very well to floral tape, cork and wax candles. All beads have been left on their original threads, but if you prefer, you may transfer the required amount of each form to a spool of fine sewing thread, using a very fine beading needle. This will eliminate the need for constantly starting new strings, and the gluing will be faster and neater. Neatness is the secret of success with this technique. If you use the original strings, be sure to start each new string of beads close to the end bead of the previously glued string. Use a moistened cloth or sponge to keep fingers free of glue.

The leaves for the artichokes, carrots, etc., and the parts for the peas and lima beans use methods already outlined in my two previous books *The Art of Making Bead Flowers and Bouquets* and *New Patterns for Bead Flowers and Decorations*. For example, the carrots are trimmed with Anemone leaves, employing continuous loops, and the artichokes use leaves in several sizes using the Basic Technique. Following are the patterns and materials needed for each.

EGGPLANT

Materials

17 strands of purple transparent beads
3½ strands of light green transparent beads
1 pear-shaped styrofoam form, 3½" by 3"
1 piece of 16-gauge stem wire, 5" long
Twig floral tape
Green floral tape
26-gauge silver spool wire

Cover the pear-shaped form with twig tape. Cover the 16-gauge stem wire with green tape. Insert one end of the stem wire into the top of the form for 2½". Wrap the open end of the bead thread around the base of the stem wire to secure, then glue beads around and down the form until the form is completely covered with purple beads.

Calyx

Basic: 7 beads, pointed top, round bottom, 7 rows.
Work with a generous basic loop, trim off top wires as usual, and tape the bottom wires with green tape for ½". Tape the stems of 3 leaves together. Repeat for the remaining 3 leaves. Tape one group of 3 leaves to one side of the 16-gauge stem wire and the other 3 leaves to the opposite side of the stem, setting both groups of leaves close to the top of the eggplant, right sides facing out. Tape all top wires, trim away leaf wires so that they do not extend beyond the 16-gauge wire. Glue light green beads around the stem, and curve the stem when the glue is dry. Make the 6 leaves in green.

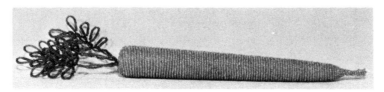

CARROTS

Materials

1 bunch orange iridescent beads
3 or 4 strands of light green transparent beads
1 orange candle, 8″ long
26-gauge spool wire

Leaves

Transfer the light green beads to a spool of 26-gauge wire and crimp the open end of the wire. Push 1″ of beads to the crimped end of the wire. This will make the first half of the stem of the leaf. Four inches from the crimped end of the wire, measure another 1″ of beads and form it into an oval loop. Push 7 beads to the base of the beaded loop, measure another 1″ of beads, form it into an oval loop, push 7 more beads to the base of the second loop, etc., until you have 7 loops, each one separated by 7 beads. At the completion of the 7th loop, fold the loops in half so that loop 1 is opposite loop 7, twist the bottom wires together twice, close to the base of the loops. Turn the leaf upside down. Push the first 1″ of beads to the base of the bottom loops, measure another 1″ of beads to the first 1″ of beads and twist together the 2 wires at the open end of the two parallel 1″ rows of beads. Give the rows of 7 beads that are between each pair of loops, one half twist, and angle all loops upward. Make 2 or 3 leaves for each carrot. Bunch the leaves, and twist their bare stem wires together, tightly, for 1″. Cut away excess wire. Heat the wires with a match or cigarette lighter and push the 1″ of twisted wires into the top of the candle.

Candle

Use either the original threads of the beads, or transfer the entire bunch to a spool of sewing thread, using a fine beading needle. Starting at the top of the candle, wrap the open end of the beaded thread around the base of the leaves, securing the thread with a bit of glue. Glue the beads around and down the candle, all the way to the bottom, including the wick that protrudes at the bottom of the candle. Cut off excess thread close to the last bead when the glue is completely dry. Glue only an inch or so at a time, giving the glue a chance to dry.

ARTICHOKES

Materials

> 3 bunches of medium green transparent beads
> 26-gauge spool wire
> green floral tape

Unit 1

Basic: 10 beads, pointed tops, round bottoms, 7 rows.
Do not remove the top basic wires, as they will be used in assembly. Twist together the bottom wires of each leaf and tape them to the end. Make 6.

Unit 2

Basic: 10 beads, one bead pointed top, round bottom, 9 rows.
Make 10 and trim off the top basic wires as usual. Twist the bottom wires of each leaf and cover with tape.

Unit 3

Basic: 5 beads, one bead pointed top, round bottom, 13 rows.
Make 12, trim off top basic wires, and tape bottom wires as usual.

Unit 4

Basic: 5 beads, one bead pointed top, round bottom, 15 rows.
Make 12, trim off top wires and tape bottom wires as usual.

Assembly

Stack 3 leaves of unit 1, one on top of the other, tops even, right sides up, and twist the top basic wires together, close to the top of the leaves. Cut away all but 1″ of the twisted wires and swing the 3 leaves into a half circle. Repeat with the remaining 3 leaves of unit 1 and swing them into a half circle. Combine the two sets of leaves

184

by stacking them, one on top of the other, tops even, right sides *in*. (back to back) Tape the top basic wires together. Reverse the leaves, bring the bottom wires together, bowing out the 6 leaves to form an elongated ball shape. Tape together the bottom wires of all 6 leaves. The top basic wires should be inside the hollow ball of leaves. Shape all leaves of the remaining units by curving them outward, slightly, and bending the tips inward, ever so slightly.

Attach a piece of green tape to the stem of unit 1, measuring ¾" below the bottom of the leaves. Tape 5 leaves of unit 2 around the stem, spacing them evenly. Tape down the stem for ¼" and add the remaining 5 leaves of unit 2, alternating them so that they are in between the first 5. Tape down for another ¼" and add the leaves of unit 3 in the same way. Repeat with the leaves of unit 4. Add all leaves right sides out. When all leaves have been added, tape the stem for 1½", cut away excess wires and cover open end with tape.

RADISHES

Materials

    1 cork or styrofoam ball, 1" in diameter
    2½ strands red transparent beads
    2 strands medium green transparent beads
    1 strand white alabaster or opaline beads
    white flower tape

Leaves

Basic: 10 beads, round top, round bottom, 3 rows.
At the completion of the 3rd row, work 2 loop-backs of beads on each side, the 1st one on the left, 2nd one on the right, 3rd one on the left, and the 4th one on the right. Measure 2" of beads for each loop-back. Twist the bottom wires together and tape them. Tape the wires of 2 or 3 leaves together, allow 2" of stem, and trim off the remaining wires. Glue the combined wires into the top of a 1" cork.

Radish

Glue on red beads, starting at the base of the leaves. Work the red beads for approximately ⅔ of the way down the ball, then change to white beads for the remainder. For the root, cover an oval wooden toothpick with white tape and insert it into the bottom of the radish, securing it with a bit of glue.

185

GREEN PEPPER

Materials

1½ bunches medium green transparent beads
26-gauge spool wire
32-gauge lacing wire
green floral tape

Leaves

Basic: 3", pointed tops, pointed bottoms, 11 rows.
Make 9 in green, and do not trim off the top basic wires of the leaves.

Lace all 9 leaves together, right sides up, in two places, 2" down from the top and 2" up from the bottom, starting, as usual, on the basic row of beads, then lacing to the outer edges. Shape the leaves outward from the inside, right sides out, twist the top basic wires together and swing them to the center of the hollow pepper. Join the 2 sets of lacing wires to close the pepper, twisting the pairs of wires together for ½". Cut away all but ¼" and tuck the ¼" of twisted wires inside the hollow pepper. Combine the bottom stem wires by twisting them tightly, then tape them for 2". Cut away all but 1½" of the taped wires, tape the open ends of the wires and push the stem toward the center of the hollow pepper until you have formed a slight indentation in the top of the pepper. Indent the bottom of the pepper, slightly, also, with your fingertips.

LIMA BEANS

Materials

2 strands light green transparent beads
3 strands pale green alabaster beads
26-gauge spool wire
32-gauge lacing wire
light green floral tape

Pod

Basic: 3", pointed top, round bottom, 11 rows.
Curve the basic wire to the right as you work. Trim off the top basic wire, as usual, at the completion of the last row, and twist the bottom wires together to form a stem. Tape the stem and cut away all but 1½" of the wires. Lace the pod in 2 places, right side up. Secure

186

the lacing wires to the outer rows of beads, and trim off the excess, close to the beads. Make 1 pod in light green transparent.

Beans

Transfer a strand or two of pale alabaster green beads to the spool of wire. Two inches from the crimped end of the wire, make a loop with 15 beads. Squash the 15 bead loop, from top to bottom, to form a narrow, horizontal loop of beads. (For detailed instructions, see Wild Pansy in *New Patterns for Bead Flowers and Decorations*). Wrap beaded wire around the outside edge of the narrow loop of beads, securing the 2nd row of beads by wrapping bare spool wire around the wire at the base of the original 15-bead loop. Wrap twice more, securing the rows of beads each time, thus giving the bean 4 rows of beads in all. Twist the bottom wires together and cover the combined wires with light green tape for ½". Trim away excess wires. Make 2 for each bean, stacking 2 together, bottoms even and taping the bottom wires together. Make 3 or 4 beans for each pod. Shape the pod, right side up, and glue the beans in a row, down the center.

GREEN PEAS

Materials

4 strands light green transparent beads
26-gauge spool wire
32-gauge lacing wire

Pod

Basic: 1½", pointed top, round bottom, 9 rows.
Make 2 in light green and trim off the top basic wires, as usual. Lace the 2 leaves together, right sides up, in 2 places. Using the basic row of beads as the starting point for the lacing, start 4 beads down from the top for one lacing, and 4 beads up from the bottom for the 2nd lacing. Do not join the lacing wires unless you want a closed pod. Instead, secure them to the outside rows of the leaves and cut away the excess close to the outer rows of beads.

Calyx

Basic: 5 beads, pointed top, round bottom, 5 rows.
Make 2 for each pod in light green, remove the top basic wires as usual, and twist the bottom wires together on each.

Pea

Basic: 2 beads, round top, round bottom, 8 rows.

Shape these like the small beehive that is used for the center of the daisies in the daisy jacket pattern. Twist bottom wires together, cut them short and turn the twisted wires into the center of the wrong side of the beehive. Make 3 or 4 in light green for each pod.

Assembly

Combine the bottom wires of the 2 leaves that make up the pod, and tape them. Tape on the 2 calyx leaves, right sides in, close to the base of the pod, and tape the wires to the end. Trim off all but 1½″ to 2″ of the wires. Shape the pod, and into one half of the pod, glue 3 or 4 peas.

For a closed pod, eliminate the peas, shape the pod, fold it in half, right sides out, twist the lacing wires together, trim off all but ¼″ of the lacing wires and tuck the ¼″ of wires into the center of the hollow pod. Tape the bottom wires, add 2 calyx, and coil the taped stem wires around a pencil or small paintbrush handle.

MUSHROOMS

Materials

> 5 strands white alabaster or opaline beads
> 1 half of 1 styrofoam ball, 1½″ in diameter
> ¾″ piece of cardboard tubing, ½″ in diameter
> white floral tape

Cut a 1½″ styrofoam ball in half, and cover it with white tape. Glue one end of the cardboard tubing to the center of the underside of the half ball. Allow it to dry completely, then cover the entire half ball and the stem with beads.

TOMATO

Materials

> 8 strands of red transparent beads
> 2½ strands medium green transparent beads
> 3″ piece of 16-gauge stem wire
> red floral tape
> green floral tape
> 26-gauge spool wire

Cover the styrofoam ball with red tape and glue red beads over the entire ball.

Calyx

Transfer 2½ strands of medium green beads to a spool of 26-gauge wire and make 8 continuous 4-row crossover loops, measuring 3″ of beads for the initial loop. Twist the end wires together close to the base of loops 1 and 8, thus forming the 8 loops into a circle. Cover the piece of 16-gauge stem wire with green tape and insert one end of the stem wire into the center of the beaded loops for 1½″. Tape beaded loop wires to the stem wire for 1″, and trim away any excess spool wire. Insert one end of the heavy stem wire into the center of the beaded ball until the beaded loops are close to the beaded ball. Shape the calyx loops upward and bend the exposed 1½″ of stem wire slightly, to form the stem of the tomato.

CORN

Materials For Ear

> *8 strands butterscotch or deep yellow transparent beads*
> *11 strands yellow opaque beads*
> *1 wax candle, stout size, 7½″ high, 1½″ in diameter at the*
> *bottom*
> *cotton sewing thread*
> *1 fine beading needle*
> *small paintbrush*
> *Elmer's glue*

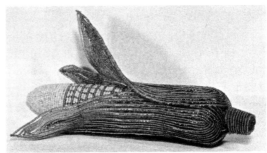

For Corn Husks

> *8 strands of lime green transparent beads for each leaf*
> *26-gauge silver spool wire*
> *32-gauge silver spool wire for lacing*

Ear of Corn

Cut off the bottom 1″ of candle, and trim off the wick at the top. Starting at the top of the candle, glue on yellow opaque beads for approximately 16 rows, using the original thread. Attach a fine beading needle to 2 yards of the thread and knot the opposite end of the thread. * Pre-string 1 butterscotch bead, 4 yellow opaque beads, 1 butterscotch bead, 4 yellow beads, etc., until you have enough to complete 2 rows of beading around the candle. You will need about 24 repeats of the pattern, depending on the size of the candle. Glue on these 2 rows, starting at the last bead of the solid yellow rows. String enough butterscotch beads for 1 row around. Repeat from * for about 2½″ down the candle, finishing with a row of butterscotch beads. For the remainder of the candle, change the pattern to 3 rows of alternating beads, then a row of butterscotch. When you have worked to the bottom of, the candle, finish off with enough butterscotch beads to cover the bottom of the flat part of the candle. Two yards of thread will not be enough to work the entire length of the candle, therefore, when you run out of thread, start again with another 2 yards of thread. Longer pieces tend to tangle. Keep the butterscotch beads that are in the pattern as vertical as possible. Trim away any knotted threads when completely dry.

Corn Husks

Basic: 5″, pointed tops, round bottoms, 19 rows.
Transfer the 8 strands of beads to a spool of 26-gauge wire. Reverse wrap the wire at the bottom of the husks as you work. On one side you will have a right side at the pointed top and a wrong side at the bottom. Turning the husk over, it will be just the opposite, wrong side at the top and right side at the bottom. Lace each husk in 2 places. For the top lacing, lace with the pointed end of the husk facing right side up and start the lacing wire on the basic row of beads 2½″ down from the top point of the leaf. For the bottom lacing, lace with the bottom of the husk facing right side up, and start the lacing wire on the basic row of beads 2½″ up from the bottom of the husk. Secure the lacing wires and clip off excess close to the beads. Trim off the top basic wire as usual, and tape the bottom wires. Make 3 or 4 husks for each ear of corn.

When attaching husks to an ear of corn, tape a 1″ piece of cardboard tubing and glue it to the center of the bottom of the candle. Use the size tubing that is found on wire clothes hangers. (same size as for mushrooms) When the glue is completely dry, tape the leaves around the base of the corn and the cardboard tubing. The bottom of each husk should be wrong side in and the tops right side in. Trim away excess husk wires at the bottom of the tubing and glue green beads around the cardboard stem.

190

INDEX